Praise, criticism, and discussion of *Old Tractors and the Men Who Love Them*:

"*Old Tractors* will keep you up half the night laughing. . . .
I believe he is the modern-day Will Rogers."
—Dave Mowitz, *Successful Farming*

"The first fact to be gleaned from [*Old Tractors* . . .]:
There is a little-known gene in a male's brain that may lie dormant
for years, but when awakened will lead to the sporadic hoarding of
iron and related memorabilia such as parts manuals, magnetos,
and needle-nose pliers."
—Barb Wilhelm, *Lincoln Journal Star*

"Forget *The Bridges of Madison County*:
Clint Eastwood and Meryl Streep it isn't."
—Dave Howe, *Nebraska Farmer*

"[*Old Tractors*. . .] does for unsticking the motor in your 1935
Allis-Chalmers WC what Verlyn Klinkenborg's 'Making Hay' did for
America's hay harvest and John McPhee's 'Building a Birch Bark Canoe'
did for birch-bark canoes."
—Dave Woods, *Minneapolis Star Tribune*

"A delightful tale of what makes gearheads tick."
—*Book Page*

"Our cultural romance with tractors has developed so far that they are
often viewed as old friends or pets:
see Roger Welsch's *Old Tractors and the Men Who Love Them*."
—*The Dynamics of Folklore*

*A case study in tractor restoration
day by day,
mistake by mistake,
disaster by disaster,
scar by scar.*

ROGER WELSCH

Busted Tractors and Rusty Knuckles

Norwegian Torque Wrench Techniques and Other Fine Points of Tractor Restoration

By Roger Welsch

Motorbooks International
Publishers & Wholesalers ®

For my beloved Linda . . .
All that talk about Cindy Crawford was just me joking around, honey . . .
No kidding . . . She doesn't mean a thing to me!

First published in 1997 by Motorbooks International Publishers &Wholesalers, 729 Prospect Avenue, PO Box 1, Osceola, WI 54020-0001 USA

On the front cover: Roger Welsch tackling the engine from his latest mission of mercy, the rescue of an Allis-Chalmers WD-45, in his shop on his tractor-strewn farm in Dannebrog, Nebraska. *Lee Klancher*

On the back cover: The Dannebrog wrecking crew gathers to celebrate the rejuvenation of The Woodpecker, another neglected Allis WC saved from the junk heap. From left to right: Dennis "Bondo" Adams (white shorts); Jim Stromp (blue coveralls); Dan Selden (blue overalls and beard); Roger Welsch; Jerry Obermiller (white hat); and Mick Maun (orange t-shirt). NOTE FOR DETAIL HOUNDS: This photograph was taken at a reenactment of the original party due to the fact that the photographer used the lame excuse of a wedding (his own) to miss the original event. Painstaking effort was taken to recreate every detail for this image: The Woodpecker roared into Dannebrog, champagne was served, and a fine time was had by all (except for Eric the bar guy, who would have preferred to be home watching television). *Lee Klancher*

Library of Congress Cataloging-in-Publication Data

ISBN 0-7603-0301-0

Printed in the United States of America

Contents

Acknowledgments

I OFTEN WONDER IF READERS UNDERSTAND HOW IMPORTANT the acknowl-
edgment section of a book is. Those heartfelt expressions of gratitude are
not, you know, just gestures; in my case, when I say, "This book would
not have been possible without the help of . . .," I mean it. And although
I have said it already a dozen times, no one deserves more thanks than
Lovely Linda, my wife. Her constant support, kind criticism, and love are
at the heart of everything I do.

Beyond that, I owe specific gratitude to Lee Klancher, Motorbooks
editor, who manages to maintain his wit and humor through even the
most difficult problems; my son Chris, who served as the master proof-
reader for the text—in fact, if you spot any problems at all with the book,
it's his fault; Verne Holoubek, who reminds me more often than he knows
what is really important; Dave Mowitz, editor at *Successful Farming*, probably the single most important figure in the growth of America's new love
for old tractors and who has been kind and generous with his help to me;
Jim Stromp, a good friend and help in my tractor work and the impetus
for this book with his gift of The Woodpecker and its accompanying
challenge; all of the "Orange People," from Nan Jones, editor of *The Old
Allis News* and Queen of the Old Allis World to every nameless bolt-
twister who ever breathed in Persian Orange paint dust or tasted
crankcase oil from an engine unopened for more than 20 years; and finally, to all those mechanics, skilled or feckless, veteran or tyro, local or at
sea, modern or throwback, ancient or adolescent who have helped me
become what I am these past six years . . . sometimes only by asking my
advice and giving me the momentary impression that I actually know
what I am doing.

Or not.

> Life's scoring system works like this: one point each
> time you learn something, two points each time you learn
> something no one else knows, three points when you learn
> something you thought you knew is wrong.
>
> —George Schwelle, *Visions*

Introduction

I STARTED THIS BOOK THINKING THAT A CASE STUDY of one man's work with
one old tractor might be of use to others. I ended this book knowing it.
My thought throughout the two years of my work with the tractor I call
The Woodpecker always has been, "Boy, I wish this book would have been
available when I got started with this tractor thing. Sure would have made
my life a lot easier." There are plenty of books telling how to do things,
how things are supposed to go, how things go best, but there is precious
little in print telling how things actually go—in part, I suspect, because
there aren't many folks who are ready to put their cards on the table and
admit to mistakes.

Not me. This book is non-fiction in the most intense sense of that
word. An expert mechanic will read this book and be astonished. He or
she will know days before I do where I screwed up, what I should have
done, how I could have saved days and days, sometimes weeks, maybe
months worth of time. He/she is going to snort at my cosmic innocence,
if not ignorance, when it comes to tools, processes, procedures, engines,
carbs, mags, the workings of the simplest mechanical devices and
machines, everything.

And he/she will be absolutely right. I am a beginner. I started working
on old tractors just 7 years ago. Up to the time I opened the brake cover
on a 1937 Allis WC that had been sitting on my farm for 15 years, I'd
never so much as changed the oil in a car. I have now dismantled maybe
15 Allis WCs (but no other kind of engine or tractor, so my experience in
terms of variety is very narrow) and I've rebuilt 10 engines and transmissions and tractors in general. That's not many, especially since a real
mechanic does that much in a week or two. The first time I rebuilt an Allis
Chalmers engine, just getting one stuck piston loose took me three
months. Now I can completely dismantle a stuck engine in a couple of

days. Thing is, I'm learning. And that's what I want to share with you in these pages—the processes of learning. It doesn't matter that I am working with Allis Chalmers WC tractors and you have a John Deere B. The tractors may be different but the agonies of learning are the same.

Every time I open an engine or take apart an Allis frame, I am surprised . . . not always pleasantly. I hope that's clear: I am not representing myself in this case study as an expert. And that's the point. Most of you are novices too. There are more beginners than experts, after all. I like to think of us as "the mortal majority." I hope this book will help you feel better about your own struggles and travails. I hope you'll be cheered, realizing that you are not a particularly inept doofus but just a plain, ordinary, run-of-the-mill doofus. I hope you'll read about my mistakes and be able to tell yourself (and maybe your spouse), "Hey, I may just be starting with this John Deere of mine, but I certainly am not dumb enough to make a mistake like this Welsch guy just made with his Allis!" That's fine with me. There's no doubt in my mind that you're not that dumb. You can't possibly be less experienced than I am.

Maybe this book is even an anti-case study. As often as I suggest what you should do, I tell you what you should avoid doing. If you read it and learn about the kinds of mistakes I make, maybe you'll be able to avoid them. Books by experts don't always do that.

Because I am something of a public figure (in a very modest way, to be sure), and because I have made a lot of my affection for old tractors, I get a lot of mail about my efforts. By and large, a good 98 percent of the time, whether they are Greenies (the John Deere faithful) or Orangemen (True Believers in the Almighty Allis), the folks who talk to me, write to me, or write about me are very helpful, giving me information I'd never pick up any other way. And often with a style of writing that makes their letters darn near literature.

In fact, some of those letters have been so interesting and/or helpful, I've decided to include them here as sidebars, so you can enjoy them and profit from them, too. I thank the good folks who have taken the trouble to write and for letting me reproduce their words here for others' benefit.

I should also warn you that this is not an absolutely accurate account of everything I did with this tractor. There are folks out there in the world whose lives consist of lying in wait, dreaming of pouncing on writers, television reporters, experts, consultants, lecturers, teachers, and coaches the moment anything comes along that—the reader or viewer—knows the "expert" has wrong. So, if you are reading along in

this text and somehow realize I wrote that I removed the magneto, but I have never reported putting it back on, and I am now trying to tell you that I started that machine, even though I never put a magneto on it, save your breath or, as the case may be, ink. It is entirely possible there are things I did with The Woodpecker restoration that did not make their way into these pages. It doesn't matter, take it from me. If it runs, I put the magneto on.

Before delving into magnetos and power take-offs, however, let me tell you a little about The Woodpecker and how she came to reside for a year and a half in my shop. She sat for 35 years in a wood lot, rusting, stuck, ruined, and getting worse. She was probably given up for dead when the farmer parked her there; the case was even more a certainty by the time she was dumped unceremoniously in the grass beside my shop.

The path she took to my shop in Dannebrog, Nebraska, is not a straight one. It actually began about 20 years ago, when a friend gave me a running 1937 Allis WC for work around my farm. It ran faithfully for years, and I'd never so much as changed her oil or greased her or checked the oil in her air cleaner. I hated mechanicking and engines and did nothing with any sort of vehicle except maybe change a flat tire, and not even that if I could avoid it.

Then, almost by mistake, I acquired another tractor of exactly the same sort, and for reasons only the Gods of Iron understand, one warm Nebraska day I decided to drain the oil pan and check a faulty brake. Something happened in a matter of minutes that day, and I was hooked.

All at once, with no warning detected by anyone, I became a tractor mechanic of sorts. I acquired other tractors, all of the same breed—Allis Chalmers WCs. It's not that they are special in any particular way or that I have some connection with Allises. That's just the way it happened.

Well, I bought three WCs one day at Jim Stromp's salvage yard in Spalding, Nebraska, to dismantle for parts for another I was rebuilding—my first shop effort, a machine I called "The Giltner," after the Nebraska town where I found it. Strompy and I discussed prices for a while and finally got pretty close to a final figure. Then, by way of a last bargaining chip, I said, "Okay, Jim, I'll pay your price . . . if you throw in the old WC down behind the combines, the one where someone painted 'Silent Orville' on the gas tank."

Jim looked at me blankly. He was baffled. He knows his salvage yard like the back of his hand, but he couldn't recall an Allis WC down by the combines with "Silent Orville" painted on its gas tank. So, finally, I took him down to the tangle of combine innards and sheet metal and showed him the rusting hulk of that WC, half buried in the sand.

He looked at it, laughed, and said, "Sure. You can have it."

A year later I had a party up at our town's tavern, celebrating the remarkable fact—remarkable, anyway, for everyone who knows me and my mechanical skills—that I had actually and indeed gotten The Giltner working. I had good reason to be proud. The Giltner was a great project—I am its second owner and the engine was stuck but good, and I still got it going. A lot of buddies had done their part in getting me through the basics of engine repair. I wanted to thank them, so I invited them to join me in the celebration. My idea was that we would sit in the tavern eating good food and drinking cheap champagne, with the front door propped open so we could listen to The Giltner run out in the street. And that's what we did.

But Jim Stromp, one of the honored guests, stood up during the toasts of the evening, raised his glass, and said, "Rog, you may have gotten The Giltner running, but listen up . . . you'll never get Silent Orville running."

Perhaps it was the champagne, perhaps it was the thrill of the challenge, but I stood up and accepted the challenge. I threw Jim's gauntlet back into his face, and announced defiantly, "Next year at this time, we'll meet again right here, drink champagne, and listen to Silent Orv run, Jim Stromp, and that's a promise."

I worked all year on Silent Orville, and by golly, the next year, roughly the same time, we had another champagne party, recommissioning "Silent Orville" as "Roaring Orv." It was a splendid party, a moment of rare triumph and glory, except for one thing: Strompy wasn't there. He was the one guy who should have been. I had sent him an invitation. He just didn't show up.

We ate, drank, gave toasts, listened to Orv's engine run, and then . . . then the tavern went dark as a huge truck rolled down Dannebrog's main street and stopped right in the middle of the street, smack in front of the tavern. It was Jim Stromp, and he called me out into the street, just like the gunfighters of a century before. I went out the door into the August sun. And there, on the back of Jim's big salvage truck, was the ugliest Allis WC I'd ever seen . . . for that matter, that I've ever seen to this day. It was wrapped in a crumpled envelope of rusting sheet metal that had once been a two-row corn picker. It was covered with dirt, leaves, broken branches, shredded bark, and rotting wood, evidence of its long years sitting idle in a farm woodlot.

"What the hell is that thing on the tractor, if that is a tractor?" someone asked.

"I think it's a corn picker," said someone else.

Someone—I think it was me—said, "Looks more like a *wood* picker, what with all that kindling hanging on it," and at that moment the rusting hulk came to be known as The Woodpecker. As the crowd continued to admire the tractor, or maybe admire that Jim had managed to winch the wreckage that had once been a tractor up onto his truck, Jim again threw down his challenge. "Rog," he said, "You got the Giltner running, and you got Roaring Orv running, but you'll never . . . NEVER . . . get this thing running!"

"Next year," I snarled. "Same time, same place, another party. She'll be running, all right."

Well, things didn't go quite that smoothly with The Woodpecker. For one thing, I spent a couple months working hard to promote my book on tractor restoration for Motorbooks, *Old Tractors and the Men Who Love Them,* and I wound up with too much other work too, so I started alibi-ing that what I had meant all along was a *metric* year, roughly twice the length of the standard King James year. I suppose I lost some time keeping this journal too. But that's okay. I'm not in this tractor work thing for efficiency or profit. I do it for fun. And two years of fun is simply twice as much fun as a single year. Right?

So, this book is the story of those months of working on The Woodpecker. It took me almost two months to figure out how to drop the corn picker off the tractor, and dragging it into the shop was a ferocious job because the tractor was no longer a vehicle; it was simply a mass of rusted, ruined iron. Eventually it was winched into the shop and the work began, which is where this book begins.

It ends with the party celebrating the revival and renewal of this noble if not elegant piece of machinery. Sort of. Actually, I suppose there isn't really an end to the story. Just as I was finishing up The Woodpecker and this book, I got a letter from a friend of mine, John Sypal. Well, actually, from his father, Ken.

If you have read *Old Tractors and the Men Who Love Them*, you might remember the Sypals, who appear in the last couple pages. To recount briefly, I was in a Lincoln, Nebraska, bookstore at a book signing (for a different book that wasn't about tractors—but by that time I'd written about tractors in a number of magazines) when a couple of teenagers came ambling down the mall's wide gallery. I'm not crazy about young people, and these were definitely not going to be an exception. "You this guy, Roger Welsch?" one asked, looking at the sign outside the bookstore.

"Yep, that's me," hoping my perfunctory response would send them on their way.

"You write this book?" he asked, turning the book over in his hand.

"Yep." I continued signing other people's books.

"I'm rebuilding my grandfather's Allis WC," he said. This kid knew and shared my love of tractors.

All at once, I saw a different person in front of me. This wasn't a kid; it was a tractor mechanic, an Allis owner, a friend, an ally, and we talked tractors.

You can read *Old Tractors and the Men Who Love Them* for the full story, but that, briefly, is it. When *Old Tractors* was published and I was back into the bookstores signing books, I figured sooner or later, John Sypal would appear again, and I could give him a copy of the book, and I could find out how he was doing with his WC, and we could talk again about our common love objects. But that never happened. So finally I wrote John and sent him a copy of the book.

About the time I got The Woodpecker running, I got a letter from Ken Sypal, John's father. It was a little depressing, at a time when I needed something cheerful. In his letter Ken explained that John was a little embarrassed, too embarrassed to write. Because of an employment cut-back, John had some financial troubles, so there wasn't a lot of money for luxuries like old tractor parts, and not a lot of time, and certainly not money to haul the tractor into Lincoln, and . . . Well, I got the idea, and I suppose you do too.

That letter really bothered me. Mostly because Ken and John were dead wrong. That's not what tractor restoration is about. It doesn't cost anything to spend a couple weeks cleaning a head with soap and water and a little kerosene, or mending an air cleaner with a little JB Weld. There's no hurry, so rebuilding a carburetor or finding and buying a replacement can wait a year or two. Even if you can't get to the tractor to retrieve components for cleaning, repair, or fondling, you can always dig out your AC owners manual, or parts catalog, or I&T shop guide and study it until the paper starts to wear through. And there are plenty of old-timers to be grilled about Allis WCs and their peculiarities. *That's* what tractor restoration is all about. I wrote that to John and Ken. Hell, what difference would it make, really, if John doesn't get his grandfather's tractor running until he's middle-aged, 20 or 30 years from now?! Not one little bit.

I would also like to head off right here and now any notion that I am making the same mistake with this book that I made with *Old Tractors and the Men Who Love Them*. That title is offensively sexist, and I know that. Lamentably, I also know that *I* am offensively sexist. Plenty of people have told me that over the years. Perhaps I became most aware of that particular flaw in my character once when I did a television story on a young farmer/F-16 pilot.

My television crew and I visited this young man on his farm in eastern Nebraska first, talked with him about farming, took some shots of him working around the farm on his tractor at a couple miles an hour, met his stunning, cheerleader-pretty wife, and then followed him to a nearby air base. I shoehorned myself into the seat of one F-16 so I could ride along on the shoot; my crew was in a huge refueling tanker so they could shoot all of us flying in formation; my farmer subject was in his F-16. As we taxied down to the runway, the pilot of the plane I was riding in asked me if there was anything special I wanted to do while I was in this fantastic war bird, and I replied that I had heard an F-16 will go straight up.

"Oh, she'll go straight up!" he laughed.

I was crushed back into the seat as we accelerated down the runway and in moments were in the air. We climbed a couple hundred feet . . . and then, right off the end of the runway, he turned the nose straight up. We went straight up a couple miles and then leveled off—upside down! I am an avid roller coaster fan, but I have never had a ride like that, ever!

My first thought, however, was of the story we were shooting. I knew that in one of the several F-16s behind me sat my farmer/pilot getting ready to take off. I also knew we had duct-taped a "lipstick" camera to his control panel, a tiny camera facing backwards right at him. "Quick,

Colonel," I told my pilot. "Tell Tom to take off just like we did!" and I could hear him do that.

Later that night, as we reviewed our tapes in our sound man's motel room, my crew and I screamed in delight, waking people all up and down the hallways of the motel, as we watched that footage. Our lipstick camera is tiny but its quality is superb, and the lens is wide enough that we could see not only the pilot's helmeted head dead center but also the landscape and sky behind him. As he took off we saw the runway flashing away behind him, and then when he pointed his plane straight up, we saw the end of the runway roll beneath him, then the air base, then Sioux City, then Nebraska, then North America, then the world. . . . Well, okay, maybe it wasn't that dramatic, but it was dramatic enough.

"Tom's wife is going to *die* when she sees what he does for a living!" I exclaimed.

My producer laughed, "Your wife is going to die when she sees what *you* do for a living, Rog!"

The next time I talked with the pilot I repeated the line: "Tom, the footage of that take-off is spectacular. Gloria is going to die when she sees what you do for a living."

There was a pregnant pause, and then Tom said, "Well, Gloria has flown in an F-16 plenty of times. She was my crew chief during Desert Storm."

"Yeah, right, Rog, you idiot," I muttered to myself. "'Cheerleader-pretty . . .' Gloria may be cheerleader-pretty all right, but she can also dismantle and re-assemble an F-16. She is not only a master mechanic, not only more of a mechanic than you, she's more of a mechanic than anyone you know. Welsch, you are a hopelessly sexist swine."

Since then I have met plenty of women who know their way around tractors too. I've learned my lesson: the restoration of old tractors is not exclusively a man's world. There are plenty of women out there who love old iron and their shops, tools, and hours spent working on stuck bolts. This book is for those women too, God love 'em.

That's what this book is about. I hope John and Ken Sypal, and tens of thousands of other novice tractor restorers like them, men and boys, women and girls, read this book and find some encouragement from it, some new patience, a new commitment to the fun of shop work on an old machine. Take your time. Clean a part or two. Relax. Look at that old iron and think about how long it worked faithfully and patiently in the field for its owners. Now it's your turn to be faithful and patient for it.

And give her a pat on the hood for me.

Preface

MY JOURNAL STARTS ROUGHLY THREE MONTHS after Jim Stromp dumped The Woodpecker in our yard. Why so long a delay? Well, she was a surprise, that's why. I already had a tractor in the shop I'd been working on for weeks. I had to finish up some things on it (it still sits in our side yard, many years later, unfinished, only one wheel on the front axle), haul it out of the shop, and get things ready in the shop to bring The Woodpecker in. For example, dismount the monstrous, ruined corn picker wrapped around it. Things like that take time. Since I'm only a hobbyist when it comes to tractor work, I don't have a lot of time to spend on it. So, it took three months.

I have written elsewhere of the day I winched The Woodpecker into the shop, where we would share many hours together over many months. Rather than relive the pain of that moment, I'm just going to quote my own words as reproduced from my syndicated newspaper column, "Roger, Over and Out," October, 1994. Let the passage speak for itself, and you can judge as you will:

> . . . A few weeks ago I told you about the battered tractor-corn picker combination Jim Stromp gave me, along with the challenge that I'd never get the thing running. The first and biggest problem was getting the blasted corn picker off the tractor so I can get one or the other into the shop. It was such a mess, I couldn't even tell what bolts or pins might have something to do with attaching one to the other, but eventually I got it sorted out and was ready to pull the tractor away—a process that requires two people, sort of like a three-arm puller. So . . ., I asked Linda to help.

Linda and Antonia both like driving a tractor, but they also agree there is nothing worse than helping me pull one tractor with another—something about "all that yelling, screaming, and cussing." I thought, therefore, that I would try something different this time: instead of Linda pulling with the International and me sitting on the wrecked Allis, I would drive the International and she would steer the derelict.

All four tires, of course, are shot on the Allis. One of the back wheels is almost completely rusted away. The front end is stuck. The seat is rusty. The slightest touch on the steering wheel leaves a black smear on your hands. We're talking about a wreck here. Linda was not happy as she climbed aboard. She was even less happy when we started pulling. "It's tipping over, it's tipping over," she screamed. "It's okay, it's okay," I yelled back over my shoulder. The International roared and groaned, the Allis clanked and clunked, shuddered and jerked. Linda kept screaming, I kept shouting.

We finally got the Allis close enough to the shop and as we were sorting out the chains, I said, "Linda, Jim Stromp had a great idea. He says we should take photos at each step of my work on this Allis. What do you think?"

Without looking at me, she said, "I think it's a great idea. Photos like that could carry a lot of weight in divorce court."

Before I can move the tractor into the shop, I jack it up, wrestle the old rusty wheels and rotten tires off—not an easy task by any means—and then install some old iron-lug wheels from which I long ago removed the lugs. These skeleton wheels let me move the tractor around without having to deal with large, dirty, smelly rubber tires. Actually, once I get the tractor into the shop, the wheels will probably come off too and the tractor will spend most of the next few weeks—months?—up on jack stands.

Thus beginneth the text and the ballad of The Woodpecker . . ..

☙ DAY 1 ☙

Beginnings

WELSCH WEATHER REPORT

Cold, snowy, dark . . . a perfect day to be in the warm, cheery shop.

EVERY TIME I BEGIN THE LONG PROJECT of rebuilding a wrecked tractor, there is an initial moment of terror when I stand there looking at it, a mass of confusing bolts, pins, welds, wires, fittings, and pipes, and wonder where one starts. It's quite a bit like looking at a newborn child—lots of potential for just about anything and everything.

This first look is also a moment of anticipation. At the moment of diving into the project I know that for days, probably weeks, maybe even months, I will be taking various components off this poor, battered machine, and along the way anticipating what I will need to do when I start putting her back together. I've done this often enough now that I no longer worry about what to do when a nut won't come off or what happens when I break a bolt, stud, or fitting. I don't like such complications, and I try to avoid them, but they happen. They're not disasters. Rather than spend energy worrying or cussing, I splash a little penetrating oil on the offender, tap it a couple of times with a hammer, and move on. (I've tried about every kind of penetrating oil but right now I'm enamored of Kano Labs Kroil. The stuff is amazing.) I can worry about shaking loose the stuck threads days, weeks, months from now.

For one endless moment I stand and stare. Her life, my life will never be the same after I begin this day, after all. We're about to get to know each other, real well. There are a thousand places I could start. A thousand things to be done.

And they all will be done. But at this stage, I take care of easy things first. Two long pipes, supports for the corn elevator I left lying on the grass out behind my shop, extend back from the rear axle; for the moment they are flopped forward onto the tractor seat. The pins holding them are hopelessly worn and rusted. No sense in even trying to save them. I cut them off quickly and easily with a hacksaw, stacking the elevator support pipes in the corner. Man, it's going to be a long time before I have to worry about them again, I think—the whole span of time it takes me to dismantle, clean, repair, replace, and re-assemble this entire machine!

I spread a drop cloth (an old sheet Lovely Linda passed along to me from her linen closet) under the tractor to keep my shop just a little on the clean side and as I move around the tractor, assessing problems, I pick away at great clumps of grease and dirt with a sharpened putty knife, letting the dirt drop onto the sheet. (Hint: I sharpen my tractor-cleaning putty knives not only on the blade but also on one side so I can scrape sideways as well as while pushing.) I toss the oily, greasy dirt out onto our driveway later in the day—ready-made asphalt!

I carry side cutters in my overall bib pocket because at this stage a major job is taking yards and pounds of baling wire off every part of the tractor. Some of the wire still holds parts on, some of it used to hold on parts that are now gone, and some of it is nothing more than tinsel on the tree. I find bent nails replacing lost cotter pins. Broken bolts flop loosely in holes where they once held something, or where they were simply stuck to keep them from clogging up the farmyard, I suppose. From Woodpecker that day, I cut off a full two-gallon bucket of wire and scrap bolts and nails.

I also carry with me on this slow dance around the tractor a squirt can of penetrating oil. Hit the screws, bolts, and nuts holding on the sheet metal with a squirt of "loose-juice," as I call it . . . some on the nuts holding the manifold, and those holding the magneto, water pump, and radiator, and tap them a couple times with a brass hammer. Squirt the tire lug nuts and tap them, as well as the air cleaner mounting bolts, and gas tank mount. Tap tap tap. I have no idea how it works, but those little taps are the magic that shakes rusty threads loose.

Squirt, tap, inspect, scrape. Jeez, there it is—the first really bad news: a long crack along the carburetor side of the block, from the drain plug at the front, clear back to the air cleaner. Someone forgot to drain the coolant from the block one late autumn day. The crack is goobered up with some kind of soft metal, maybe lead, or solder. It's a problem, but not a fatal problem. I've dealt with this before. I could probably just put in a cooling system sealer once I get the tractor running and that would hold it for my purposes, but since I'm planning to learn how to weld this winter, maybe this will be a place to think about learning how to weld cast-iron with nickel rod. If I run into other problems, I may want to replace the block. I have a couple spares. We'll see down the road—no sense in getting excited about *anything* at this point.

The screws and bolts securing the metal straps holding on the two major pieces of sheet metal on an Allis Chalmers WC, the hood and the gas tank, have always been in my experience the rustiest, most stubborn threads to break loose. I squirt on some penetrating oil, tap them a couple times, and for no particular reason give them a little twist with a large screwdriver. I'll be darned—the screws and bolts turn easily! If I have learned one thing in my short time working with old tractors, it's you can't count on anything. They may be simple but they are never predictable. Nothing is predictable on an old tractor, nothing is normal, nothing is the same from one old tractor to the next. I can't believe it: the bolts and screws are off, and with them, the sheet metal, just like that. I put the sheet metal parts aside. It'll be a long time before I have to worry about them again.

The hood is not dented, torn, or cut up. That is unusual for an Allis WC. This model tractor came originally with a manifold that poked the exhaust pipe off at a jaunty angle to the side of the tractor, out from under the hood. As the original manifolds burned and rusted out, they were replaced with newer manifolds, often from WD tractors, on which the exhaust stack pointed straight up. The only way you can mount a vertical exhaust stack on a tractor designed for a canted stack is to cut a hole somehow in the hood— in some cases with a cutting torch, in others with a cold chisel, tin snips, or hacksaw. Pretty messy work. But on Woodpecker the hood is pristine. That's nice. Eventually she'll look a lot better because of that smooth hood.

Not surprisingly, the gas tank on an old tractor often has holes in it. Water gets into the tanks in the form of condensation, if no other way, and settles to the bottom, rusting pin holes through the metal. But Woodpecker's tank looks solid and clean, too. I may wind up relining the tank with a liquid sealer anyway, just to be sure there isn't gas seeping all over things when I put it back on.

The real surprise comes when I lift the gas tank from the frames holding it. Usually there are strips of heavy woven strap between the mounting bars and the gas tank itself, but what's this?—lengths of stiff harness leather. Wow. When the farmer worked on this gas tank at some point, maybe soldering shut a hole or shaking out some junk, he replaced the old cloth padding with pieces of harness he no longer needed.

I imagine that harness was hanging there in the barn from the same nail where it had been slung the last time it was taken off old Ned and Nell before they were sold and a tractor was purchased to replace them—perhaps this very tractor. Ouch. There's a lot of story in those two pieces of dirty old leather. I hang the scraps on the wall of the shop to remind me what these machines meant to the farmers for whom they were new. This wrecked tractor I'm about to start working on wasn't simply a new piece of equipment for some farmer; it constituted a change in eras, from the Draft Animal Age to the Machine Age.

The grill comes off the front of the radiator cleanly and easily. Like the hood, it is in good condition. I hang large pieces such as the hood from heavy nails and screws in the rafters above my head, take large elements like the gas tank and radiator outside the shop door into a shed where they are out of the weather. It'll be months before I get to them again, so there's no sense in cluttering up the shop floor or walls with them. As I take parts off—radiator, carburetor, transmission port—I package the screws, bolts, and nuts associated with them in clear plastic bags and fasten them securely to the component with thin wire ties or tape, even if they are broken or rusted. The ruined pieces may help me find appropriate replacements. If not, I can always throw them away later. I label everything with magic marker, plastic tabs, notes on masking tape, or duct tape.

As I remove the throttle linkage, carburetor, and other small parts, I notice something I'll chuckle at through the process of working with this particular tractor—not a single cotter pin. Not one. Nails, wire, even a hairpin and a safety pin (the wife must have been delivering lunch out to the field when the farmer found himself in need of a cotter pin on that occasion, and even had the baby with her the next!), but no cotter pins.

The manifold is always a problem with old tractors, in large part because of the heat the parts are exposed to, I suppose. But for all the make-do nature of the rest of the tractor—baling wire and nails—someone did have the decency to use brass nuts on the manifold studs. All but one come off relatively easily, therefore, before the last one twists off the stud well away from the block. Well, I can wish they had all come out easily, but one broken stud is a lot better than usual. When I pull off the manifold, I'll douse that stubborn stud well with penetrating oil, tap it a dozen times with a hammer, and hope it loosens up by the time I get to working on the manifold again in a couple months. Then I can put it on the bench, bang at it a little more comfortably, apply a little heat . . . it may shake loose.

Two large bolts hold the radiator to the frame from underneath. To make access a little easier I remove the right front wheel, which winds up being a lot harder than I can recall having run into before. From all the dirt caked onto the front wheels and pedestal, I get the feeling the entire front end must have been buried in the ground for some time. I've seen that happen: dirt, leaves, and junk piles up and pretty soon an entire section of the tractor is buried. And rusting.

I squirt penetrating oil on the wheel studs and twist away with a hand lug wrench. I get a couple lug nuts loose but the others don't even budge. So, what was almost going to be a simple and fast job gets complicated and lengthy. I start the air compressor, drag out the air hose and impact wrench, and bang away at the lugs. It still isn't quick and easy but after a half hour of work, I finally have the rusted, bent wheel and shreds of what was a tire off.

What I thought would be the hard part—the two rusty old bolts under the radiator—also fool me, coming off quickly and easily. I cut the radiator hose in half to free the radiator quickly; it is so rotten and the clamps so rusted, there's no sense in trying to save either. I haul the radiator out to the shed after looking it over. Not bad. This tractor that came to me as a kind of joke because it was so utterly disreputable is turning out to be in better shape than I had feared. Old Jim Stromp might kick himself for giving her away by the time this is all over.

Once the radiator is off, it's easy to get at the water pump and with a breaker bar and ratchet, the three bolts that hold it turn right out of the block. It's hard to tell from looking at it, but the fan rotor seems firm, so maybe the seals and bearings in it are okay. I'll be able to tell more later. Again, it'll be a while before I have to worry about this particular component.

About this time Kenny Porath, a professional mechanic friend, comes into the shop to work on the hydraulics system of my working farm tractor, an International 300. We've been talking about draining the hydraulic oil out for a long time, and installing a new drain plug, but of course we put it off almost until it was too late. If it snows much more, I'm going to have to have that tractor to plow our way out of the farm, and if the water in the hydraulic oil freezes up yet again . . . well, there'll be no plowing. So, Kenny decides it's time we jump on this job, cold and snowy or not.

We drill, tap, and plug the International 300, retreating now and then to the shop to warm our hands. While we're thawing out toes and fingers, Kenny looks over what's going on with The Woodpecker. Actually, I'm surprised the first time we come back into the shop: I began this morning and have only been working about four hours but already the tractor is almost completely stripped down. It's already more a carcass of a tractor than the pile of scrap iron it was. The project is moving along fast.

Kenny notes the cracked block. "Let me know when you're ready to work on that block. Clean it up real good and I'll come over with some cast-iron rod and we'll get that fixed up so you can't even tell it was ever split." I'm a long ways from worrying about the block, but it's nice to know that when the time does come, the problem is already well along the way to being solved!

Kenny and I finish the job on the International and I plod through the snow back to the house for supper. Since I left the shop pretty much in a shambles, I excuse myself from Linda and my daughter Antonia after supper. "I'll be back in an hour," I explain.

Actually, I should spend more evenings in the shop; if the shop is warm and cozy during the day, it's even more so at night. I clean up and put away the tools I've used during the day, put away some parts, and sweep up under The Woodpecker, wondering what she must think, getting all this attention after being ignored for so long. (And don't think I'm being cute; these old tractors have a life and soul to them, as anyone who has worked on them will tell you. I thought I was going out on a limb the first time I suggested the notion of an old tractor having life and soul, but now scarcely a week goes by that I don't hear from another old iron enthusiast saying pretty much the same thing.) Before closing up the shop, I take off the four nuts holding on the valve cover and am happy to find that everything with the rockers seems to be in pretty good shape.

Except maybe that one valve spring is completely different and clearly of a different size than the other seven. That's probably not a good idea, but it's not unusual. I guess shade tree mechanics used whatever the local parts store happened to have in stock, even if it didn't even come close to matching the originals. I spin off the four nuts holding the water manifold and take it off. What the heck, while I'm at it, and since I've only been out here a half hour, I turn off the other head nuts and pull the head off.

Again, I am pleasantly surprised. The cylinders are relatively clean. They're not at all pitted, but they do have pretty bad ridges at the top where the piston rings stopped and started back down in their mad race back and forth over the years. That can be solved easily enough with a ridge reamer, designed precisely for this problem. There's a lot of carbon on the head and pistons, but that will clean off, maybe some other cold, snowy day early this winter.

I put the head and rocker bar off to the side where they can stay clean and safe from being bent or scratched. I clean up, hang up my shop apron, turn off the lights, and walk back through the snow to the house, content with the progress I have made with the old Woodpecker in these five hours of the first day I have worked on her. I'll bet I sleep that legendary Sleep of the Innocent tonight!

What I will do through this journal, is let you know how much time I spend on each visit to the shop and how many total hours I've spent on Woodpecker. Now, don't get on my case about this. I know you've done similar jobs in far less time if you're any mechanic at all, and I am spending far too much time for what I'm getting done. I'm doing this for fun. I'm in no hurry. As an amateur I take a lot more time than a real mechanic would.

Day 1 hours	5.0
Total project hours	5.0

The Stud Seminar

I HAVE DREAMED OF HAVING TWO OR three days of tractor and shop work in a row, but that's not the way it goes in my shop, in my life. I use my shop as a carrot: "Look, you big dummy," I tell myself. "If you work hard in your office for, oh, two full days . . . *and* put in a full day taking care of 'honey-do jobs' for Linda in the house, *then* you can have a full day working in the shop." But the fact of the matter is, I won't get a full day—there's no such thing in my life as a full day without some obligation of some kind or another—but I may get a good half day now and then, and that's worth working for.

So, don't think for a moment that Day 2 is either a full day or the day immediately after Day 1 in this journal. It is actually more like a week later, as you can tell from the substantial change in weather. And, just as I predicted, it wasn't a full day either.

I have also been promising myself for the past couple weeks that I would corner my friend, town machinist Don Hochstetler, and have him give me a stud seminar (Lovely Linda was very interested in the idea of a "stud seminar" until she found out it had something to do with tractor engines). As I mentioned in my first journal entry, you just don't get a manifold out without twisting off a stud . . . or six. Not when you're working with old iron. Sure, I would rather have time to work in the shop than sit in town talking—even when it's an old friend like Don, but a couple hours spent with Don could easily save me many hours in the shop somewhere, probably often, down the line.

As Don has done with me before, on shifters, magnetos, and carbs, he generously takes the time to sit me down and show me exactly what he does when he twists off a stud: penetrating oil and tapping. (He added to Mel Grim's advice I got the first day I started tinkering with old tractors, however, recommending that I tap on the casting *around the stud* as well as on the stud itself.) He drills directly down the middle of the stud with a reverse twist bit, hoping the heat and torque might turn the stubborn stud out (it rarely does on old tractors, but it's worth a try, because you're going to have to drill a hole in the center of the broken stud anyway so what does it matter which direction the drill bit is turning?), blow some heat through the bolt with a welding torch, propane torch, or carbon arc torch (although Don doesn't advise this because he believes the carbon tends to weld the stuck iron in its hole rather than loosening it), try twisting again while the iron is hot, try an EZ Out, and then cuss like crazy when it breaks off, which it will always do, and finally burn it out with the torch. Don shows me all the steps and sends me home with two manifolds to work on for practice.

But I don't get to the practice. I decide instead to jack up the tractor and set it on solid jack stands so I won't have to be uneasy working around it the next year or so. I put two commercial jack-stands under the back and 6x6 post sections under the front. Solid as a rock. I shake the remaining front wheel to see how firm the axle bearings felt—just fine—and the steering pedestal to see how the main front bearing feels—a trifle loose but not bad. I'll have to see a little later if the seal in the pedestal leaks. If it does, I'll drop the steering mechanism out of the pedestal anyway; if it doesn't, I won't. I may pull the whole thing apart anyway, just to look it over and clean it up. There's no sense in cutting corners here. At this point it's the corners that are the fun.

My total time in the shop today is about an hour, not counting the stud lesson, just enough to put my soul at ease.

Day 2 hours	1.0
Total project hours:	6.0

Lost But Still Looking

The following letter from Jim Prentice is frustrating: I haven't been able to find the recommended books anywhere, and neither have any book searchers. Let me know if you can help me.

Roger,

My own affliction with tractors goes quite a bit deeper and includes most anything old made of metal—parlor stoves, one-lung engines, construction equipment, etc. Unfortunately I do not get to spend as much time with my hobby as I would like. My wife wanted to know if your book would explain this disease. I told her no, but it would give some insight to my state of mind.

But what I really wanted to tell you is this: there are two books by Keith Daniels of Lost Data Press. If you do not already have them, get them immediately. You will love them. They are titled *Hand-Made Tools 1890-1948* and *Recycling and Repairing 1912-1948.*

Mr. Daniels went through God-knows-how-many back issues of magazines and collected the letters sent in by readers to the helpful hints columns. Each book contains hundreds of ideas. Some rank right up there with putting a tire back on its rim using ether. It's true that most of the equipment built early this century was meant to be repaired in the field (sometimes literally) using common tools. But some people were much more clever with how they used their tools than others.

A favorite quote I have to remind myself of from time to time is found on the inside cover of *Hand-Made Tools.* It says simply this, "Remember: If you can't get the propeller off of the shaft, try getting the shaft out of the propeller." It's remarkable how often this works.

Their address is listed as Lost Data Press, 4410 Burnet Rd., Austin TX 78756 (512-452-0924).

—Jim Prentice

I have had no luck with this address or telephone number and I still have not acquired these books. I just wish Jim hadn't recommended them so highly!

Exit Studs, Enter Hubris

I WORK IN THE OFFICE ALL MORNING while the shop warms up and therefore don't manage to get out there until an hour before supper time. I live in constant fear of the moment someone in authority tells me I need to reconsider my priorities in life and devote more time to what's important. No doubt in my mind what that means—more shop time! Well, an hour is better than nothing.

I turn off the engine block studs, which isn't much of a job—just enough to work up a sweat, even in a cold shop. I wish I had a good stud wrench to fit them, but all mine are too small and big ones are too expensive for my tool budget, so I just use Vise Grip pliers and twist hard. I'm still picking and scraping, looking this situation over, and thinking about what sort of problems I might have in future afternoons. As I look over how far I've come so far, just a three days over a couple weeks, it is amazing how stripped down Woodpecker looks already. This is already an easier job than Jim Stromp thought it was going to be, maybe even easier than I thought.

Day 3 hours	1.0
Total project hours	7.0

Author's Note: in the world of scholarship, this sort of attitude is known as "hubris," a Greek word meaning "fatal pride." In Greek plays someone inevitably shows far too much arrogance and everyone in the audience knows that this means the gods, offended by such snot-nosed confidence, are surely going to knock the cocky smart-ass down a few pegs. Most of us know how hubris works: no one says, "It's okay if I go 10 or 15 miles over the speed limit; I haven't been stopped by the cops for years now" or "Look at the check book! We have an extra $100. We have plenty of money to get us through the end of the month." We knock on wood if we even come close to such hubris because we know that just as sure as we're human beings the next sound will be that of a police siren, and that the speeding fine will cost roughly $120. As I review these words for publication, two years have passed since I wrote the last sentence of the journal for Day Three. I should have known even then, shooting off my mouth about how easily things were going, how good The Woodpecker looked, that sort of thing, was a sure path for disaster, not to mention a short book. Don't worry. I wasn't all that lucky. You're not going to wind up being disgusted because everything goes right for me, not by a long shot! There will be plenty of misery for you to take comfort in!

Oil Pan Blues

I START THE WOOD STOVE AT 8 A.M. The stove is an old-time top-loader a buddy picked up for me for $35 at an auction sale. I burn elm cut right here on the farm, but I could probably heat the place by burning old gaskets! By noon the shop is warm enough to work in. You have to remember, when you use a wood fire to heat a shop, you have to wait too until your *iron* is warm—tools, parts, tractors, stool. Especially your stool!

I pull up the old, now filthy couch cushion I use for a creeper sometimes and sit on the floor beside the second and worst of the stuck front wheels. I scrape off as much dirt and grease as I can with my sharpened putty knife. I squirt penetrating oil on the battered lug nuts, and to my surprise they come off without having to break out the compressor and impact wrench. I continue to take covers off various compartments—clutch, transmission, brakes, that sort of thing. I drain the rear drives and transmissions—nothing coming out but water—not a good sign. I can only hope there hasn't been enough water in here over the last 20 winters to break castings, bearings, or seals. (Actually, I'll probably wind up replacing most of the seals anyway. They are the first parts to wear out and they're not all that expensive. You just about have to take out the seals to look at most bearings, so . . .)

I try to turn out the plug on the oil pan but, reminiscent of my first experience with tractor mechanics, all I do is round off the corners. As the plug gets smaller and smaller, I decide there is no hope. Since I am going to have to take off the oil pan anyway to check the oil pump, main bearings, rod bearings, and to pull the sleeves and pistons, I might just as well take the pan off now and then I'll work on it at my bench, sitting there in a lot more comfortable a position than lying on my back under the engine. All the pan bolts come out relatively easily, but I do note that a couple bolts were twisted off sometime in the past—probably a long time in the past. Happens all the time. Since the pan was obviously pretty tight without them, I could probably get by without replacing them, but what the heck—this is a good chance to practice my stuck-bolt removing techniques, so sometime later this winter, I'll try some of the tricks Don taught me up in his shop. If I can't get them out, I haven't lost anything by trying. I can always put the pan back the way it was, as much as that would annoy me.

To take the oil pan off my Allis WCs, I have to take the cover off the fly wheel where there is always a generous population of wasp nests and, in this case, a dead mouse. I also have to remove the front engine support—a length of angle iron that spans the two frame beams. The front of the engine is attached to that angle iron with two large bolts. They turn out easily on The Woodpecker. They are large, ¾-inch bolts, so I can use a large socket, a long breaker bar, and plenty of force. They are not likely to break off because they are so big; I'd rather work hard at getting things like this off whole than twist off a bolt.

The first time I did this job, I read in the shop manual about taking off the oil pan. It said something to the effect of, "Remove the front engine support and then the oil pan will drop directly from the engine block." Right, I thought. I'm going to remove the support from the engine and then lie there under it, knowing all the while that the only thing holding it up are those four bolts attaching it to the clutch housing! I think I ran a chain around the engine and over a shop beam on that occasion. I have since dismantled tractors where the front engine support was altogether gone and obviously had been gone for some time while the tractor was a working machine. I don't suppose it's good for the engine, hanging there without the front support, but I no longer worry about those four bolts holding it up.

Actually, an Allis WC engine is not all that heavy. I can't lift a whole one up, but once I take off the various fittings and parts, drop the oil pan, and pull the sleeves and pistons, I can lift the block up and carry it out to the shed easily. I suppose it weighs something like 75 pounds. Four ¾-inch bolts should hold it.

Day 4 hours	5.0
Total project hours	12.0

The Wall
of Despair

**WELSCH
WEATHER
REPORT**

Another miserable
winter day. I can't
believe my luck!

RUNNERS TALK ABOUT "HITTING THE WALL," a feeling
that comes well into a long run when suddenly
exhaustion comes on in a way that really is just like
hitting a wall. Everything goes into slow motion,
everything in you gives up, and you wonder what
the hell you're doing here, doing this stupid thing
when there are so many better things to do.

Today I hit the wall. I suppose the shock was made all the worse
because things seemed to be going so well, and so quickly. Right off the
bat, disaster struck. I was taking off the few brass oil fittings on
Woodpecker's engine block. There's not much there—an oil filter holder fastened to a heavy plate with two nuts—no problem there. (Although
I did once get this component off with no problem at all—and then
dropped it and watched it fall in slow motion and shatter on the shop
floor.) A line runs from the bottom of it to a brass T-fitting low on the
block, where oil comes up from the pump, and another line runs from it
up to a brass L-fitting on the head, which carries lubricant to the rocker
arms and valves. Remember, until a couple years ago I had never so much
as changed the oil in a car, not to mention trying to figure out how a
vehicle's oil system works. But the beauty of these old machines is that
they are so simple, even a doofus like me can figure them out with just a
little common sense, some good advice, and a couple of books.

The whole oil system on an Allis WC consists of two copper lines; how
complicated can that be? Well, it gets complicated pretty fast when you
twist off the T-fitting, which is exactly what I do at this point. I apply the
least pressure—I'd guess the fitting was cracked to begin with—and ping,
it breaks off.

The problem is, sitting low on the block, it's very hard to get at with a drill. On the other hand, it is made a little simpler by virtue of the fitting being brass and the block iron. For one thing, they expand and contract at different rates and by heating and cooling the fitting and the block around it, I may be able to loosen it enough to get it turning—if I can get something in it, I'll have something to apply pressure on.

The fitting broke off flush with the block. Reaching down alongside the inside of the frame beam, I push an EZ Out into the fitting's hole as firmly as I can. I tap it twice with a light-weight mechanic's hammer. Ping. I hear the sound, the tinkle of something hitting the shop floor, and I don't even want to contemplate what I'm sure had happened. That damned EZ Out has snapped off, *flush* in the fitting, flush with the block.

Now I really do have a problem. The brass of the fitting is soft, easy to drill, easy to move around; that EZ Out is hard as flint. Can't touch it with a drill bit. Jeez, now what? I spend the rest of the afternoon tapping with a small chisel and little hammer, trying to shake that EZ Out loose. I finally get a fraction of an inch of the brass of the fitting away from the EZ Out and with the nose of a long-nose Vise-Grip pliers manage just the slightest grip on that piece of steel, and . . . whew! I manage to get it loose . . . and out! A small victory, but a victory. I'm back where I started. I feel like the guy going into the race track saying, "I sure hope I break even today. I could really use the money."

I give up on the sheared fitting. It's just going to have to wait until I can figure out to get at it more easily. (I already know I'll either have to take off the entire frame rail—no small task—or remove the engine, probably the course of choice.) I decide to smooth out my day by taking out the pistons. The rod cap nuts come off easily, bing, bing, bing, and with relatively little effort I push three pistons out the top of the cylinder sleeves. I'm on a roll again, I figure. And the pistons don't look at all bad. The rings are in good shape, the cylinder walls are a little ridged, but not bad. All right!

I figure I'll finish this one last piston and call it a successful day . . . except for the sheared oil fitting. I take off the rod cap nuts, carefully keeping track of the shims, bearings, nuts, and bolts. It's not as important to keep everything the same in these old engines as it is in a high performance race car or airplane engine but why not be safe? I push on the last piston (which happens to be the number one piston, the front one in the engine. Hmmm. Pretty solid. I tap on it with a brass hammer. Nothing. I squirt some penetrating oil into the cylinder around the piston. I tap on it from the top with a brass rod. Judging from how easily the other pistons came out, this one should be easy too. I crawl back under the tractor and pound a little more. Nothing. No hint of movement. I get a 16-ounce hammer and give it a couple firm raps. Nothing. I hook a chain around the engine and put a hydraulic bottle jack under the engine, on the chain, with an iron rod reaching up to the bottom of the piston. Nothing. The rod bends, the jack groans. I break out a sleeve puller and extract the second cylinder liner, which opens up the inside of the block and lets me get a look at one side of the first cylinder sleeve. It's dirty and rusty but no worse than 50 others I've seen. No hint of where the problem might be. I squirt penetrating oil on it through the second cylinder hole and onto its other side through the water pump port, figuring I'm lucky it's the first cylinder because I wouldn't even have that advantage in any of the other sleeves. I rap on it with a hammer, pound on the bottom again. Neither sleeve nor piston budges.

I give up after three hours of fairly universal failure and call it a day. Not much comfort.

Day 5 hours:	3.0
Total project hours:	15.0

Tool Jewels

In *Old Tractors and the Men Who Love Them* I expressed my enthusiasm for Sears Craftsman tools (as well as for other products like the wonderful Vise-Grip series of wrenches). I noted that I have never been able to get any response at all from Snap-On or Mac tools, maybe because I don't have the kind of money it takes to play in that league. At any rate, Rick Schweizer commented:

> Roger,
>
> I really enjoyed *Old Tractors and the Men Who Love Them*. I wish I had read it when I "did" my Massey-Harris Pony. Didn't know there was so much info about old tractors out there. Some say that ignorance is bliss but I feel ignorance is blisters!

Anyway, the reason for this letter is to return the favor. Over the years I have run across most of the products you mentioned in the book. One not mentioned but worth a try is Never-Seize. It keeps things (head, manifold bolts) from getting stuck again. Just think how grateful someone 50 years from now will be when they remove head bolts from your WC without problems!

Also Mac Tools was mentioned. You couldn't contact them. Their address is Mac Tools, So Fayette St., Washington Courthouse, Ohio 43160. Good tools, less $ than Snap-On. They are sold out of tool trucks. Another line of tools I recommend is OTC. They are basically specialized tools—shop equipment. An excellent book to have in the library. The address for OTC tools is 655 Eisenhower Dr., Owatonna, MN 55060, tel: 507-455-1480, FAX: 1-800-283-8665.

In closing, may I suggest a sequel, "Women Whose Men Love Old Tractors"? It could list ways of coping and/or lists of good lawyers.

—Rick Schweizer

Man, that's a book I for one hope never to see on the market! Whew.

🚜 *DAY 6* 🚜

Pounding Pistons

WELSCH WEATHER REPORT

Another cold winter day. This is the day immediately following Day 5, a rare occurrence for me—two days in a row in the shop.

I CAN'T GET THE STUCK PISTON OFF MY MIND, but today isn't going to help, I'm afraid. I lie on the creeper under that tractor and pound up against the struck piston until my arms hurt. Nothing seems to go right. I drop the brass rod I am using to reach into the piston and it lands smack on my nose. Penetrating oil drips onto my clothes and face. This is the point where my hair gets caught under the creeper and I envision the local EMTs having to make a mercy run and rescue me from my plight until I wrench my head loose. (For the full story, see *Old Tractors and the Men Who Love Them*.)

I do what I can to bring cheer into the process—I pour two fingers of single-malt scotch—my universal brain solvent. I review the month's

obligations by studying my Pamela Lee calendar. I turn up the volume on a soothing ZZ Top number blasting on my stereo. Nothing brings cheer.

I return to the house feeling pretty grumpy. I just spent five miserable hours without the slightest sign of movement in the piston or sleeve except that pieces of the piston are starting to break off. So, the piston is ruined. Now I have to hope I haven't ruined the sleeve too.

Day 6 hours	5.0
Total project hours	20.0

Bondo
Beats the Piston

**WELSCH
WEATHER
REPORT**

Cold, sleety, icy
day.

THIS SHOULD BE A GREAT DAY IN THE SHOP but I'm still smarting from recent set-backs. I'm in the shop today not to work on The Woodpecker but to work on my Christmas hams. Every year I cure and smoke 40-plus hams for friends and family. "Curing" a ham requires a couple weeks of rubbing salt into the hams every couple days and keeping them at a temperature above freezing but not warm.

Well, the shop is the best place to do that. It cools off nights and I can stoke the stove during the day enough to keep the temperature just about right. My reasoning has always been that I can get double use out of my firewood if I use it to heat the shop for my hams because then I can also work in the shop. Even if I can't work in the shop, the heat will keep paint, solvent, and other liquids from freezing up. Today I rub the hams and pack them into their barrels to cure, only now and then glaring over at The Woodpecker with its stuck piston.

Three days later I'm back in the shop, stoking the fire, and rubbing the hams, feeling renewed, rested, and a trifle optimistic again. I crawl under the engine and start pounding at that piston again. The piston seems to give just the slightest bit, and I can see from the top of the block that I am also pushing the sleeve slightly above the block. I slather penetrating oil on the piston and the sleeve, and pound everything down back into place, which then pushes penetrating oil down into sticky parts, then pound it back up again, a trick I learned from Mel up at the service station in town.

After a couple hours of this I start to slow down again when my buddy Bondo busts through the door. "Ho, Rog, whatcha doing?"

"Well, it ought to pretty obvious, since I'm lying here under this tractor with a hammer in one hand and a brass rod in the other, covered with grease and dirt, surrounded by pieces of broken piston. I'm doing exactly what I've been doing for weeks—trying to pound out this blasted stuck piston."

"Well, there's your problem then," he says with confidence. He is walking across the shop but hasn't even looked at the engine yet. How can he so easily spot a problem I haven't seen while lying right under this thing?

"What is my problem?" I ask, now thoroughly bewildered.

"You've been pounding on the engine. You don't *pound* on old tractors. You *beat* on old tractors."

I recall immediately that every time I've had a conversation with old machinists, mechanics, farmers, or tractor nuts, that's what they say— they've been *beating* on the thing. Bondo may be right.

"Let me take a turn at it," Bondo said with a chuckle. "It's my birthday. Maybe I'll have some birthday-boy luck."

So Bondo jumps on the creeper, swings under the engine, turns the crankshaft, catches his finger between the crankshaft and the piston rod, says a few choice words real mechanics use now and then, and starts *beating* on that stuck piston. And darned if it doesn't start to break up. The whole piston skirt falls out. Then the rod. Now we can start pounding . . . er, beating . . . from the top of the piston because there is room for it to move down into the block. I drop a six-inch section of Welsch's Custom

Piston Remover (sawed off fence post) into the cylinder and use a two-pound machinist's hammer to really bang (as opposed to "beat") now that we are pounding down and have some room to swing. The remaining body of the piston drops clear and clanks to the floor.

My first concern is the sleeve—the tube in which the piston moves up and down. These things aren't cheap. For my Allises each "hole"—sleeve, rings, piston, and rod—cost about $135. They are therefore worth saving when they can be saved. But this sleeve appears to be clean, smooth, unpitted—not even rusty. So what was holding that blasted piston in there?! I pick up the shattered remnants of the piston. The rings are stuck into their grooves, but they're not corroded. They are dirty, but not rusted. In fact, they actually look fairly . . . clean!

The point is, it just doesn't take much to stick an engine. But it takes a lot to break it loose.

Bondo and I retire to the town tavern to celebrate his birthday and a major victory in the resurrection of The Woodpecker. Having seen my frustration over the past weeks, Linda understands, says good-bye, and wishes us a happy evening.

Day 7 hours:	5.0
Total project hours:	25.0

DAY 8

Reaming a Ridge

WELSCH WEATHER REPORT

Very cold, sleet, freezing rain.

I'M IN THE SHOP THIS AFTERNOON, not simply because I am again looking forward to working on Woodpecker, not simply because I need to clean up the mess from the work on the pistons, but because I am worried. Linda had to drive to another town today, about 50 miles away, and the weather has turned very nasty. On the radio the announcer keeps saying that no one should go on the highways unless they absolutely have to, and she is out there on the ice. From the shop I can see our farmyard and hear any vehicles coming in the lane, so from the vantage point of the shop, I'll know the moment she comes in.

I'm also concerned about what this freezing rain means for the rest of the day. We live on a farm out in the country. Everything in our house is run by electricity. If we lose power, we can heat the main part of the house with our fireplace, but it seems to me nonetheless that I'm overdue in taking a look at our portable generator. I drag the generator into the shop, check the oil, turn the crank to be sure it'll start, and drag it down to our back porch where it will be ready to use if the ice should bring the lines to our farm down.

Back in the shop I clean up the mess under The Woodpecker, sweep the floor, and put away tools. Linda is almost an hour late and the weather is deteriorating fast. I've checked the three sleeves still in the engine block (Remember—I pulled sleeve number two out so I could get penetrating oil on the stuck piston and sleeve number one) and two of them have prominent ridges, worn at the top of the pistons' swing. I dig out my new ridge reamer, which I have never used, and try to decipher the instructions, obviously written by some Japanese guy who took three years of English when he was a kid. But I know what a ridge reamer is supposed to do—ream the ridge!—and I remind myself of the eternal mantra, "THIS CAN'T BE COM-PLICATED!" and before long I have a pretty good idea of how the thing works.

I install it in the first cylinder, tighten it down, put a socket and ratchet on the turning nut, and start to crank her around. Darned if it doesn't cut quite smoothly, taking the ridge down noticeably. I back the reamer up, tighten it down another turn, and bring it back up to the top of the sleeve, scraping away another fraction of the metal on the unwanted ridge.

Hey, that's not bad at all! And as if on cue, I see Linda pulling cautiously across the ice of our parking slab. I welcome her home and we gasp together at the antenna on her car—converted into an icy baseball-bat by the freezing rain. Now I can relax.

The rest of the afternoon I ream ridges, dig out my sleeve puller—a homemade device fabricated for me by Plumber Dan Selden, and pull the remaining sleeves from the block—a laborious and time-consuming job but one that goes smoothly for a change. Tonight I go across the snowy, icy yard to the house feeling pretty good about the afternoon and delight-ed with the idea that tonight we'll be able to sit by the warm fire, glad we're all here, glad we're alive.

Day 8 hours:	6.0
Total project hours	31.0

More Good Advice About Stuck Stuff

Sometimes the truth is so obvious, we are struck dumb when it takes someone else to point it out to us. I wrote a book, *Diggin' In and Piggin' Out*, about men and food, mostly highly prejudiced statements about me and my tastes. One thing I do know is true is that boiling coffee makes it bit-ter, so percolators are the dumbest possible way to make coffee. The best way is to pour boiling water over the grounds. It doesn't take a genius to figure that out, and yet how many people have the good sense to make their coffee right?

Whoops. Then along comes, of all people, my friend Andy Rooney from CBS's *60 Minutes*. I watched Andy on the show of June 30, 1996, say all the stuff I know about coffee—use good coffee even though good coffee is expensive, use good water, don't boil the coffee (and therefore percolators are dumb devices) . . . But then he said something that just knocked me out: He said we should pour our good coffee grounds *into* the hot good water so the water has more than a passing chance to touch the coffee grounds, and then pour the mixture through a filter into a pot. Holy moley! A stroke of genius. Obvious as the nose on my face, and in my case that is not a metaphor, and yet I never thought of it.

The following letter from Carl W. Andersen of Edgar, Nebraska, also an old friend, is the same sort of thing. Read carefully what Carl has to say about stuck bolts. His words will help you understand them, no kidding. It's not as simple a situation as you think, not so helpless a matter as you fear—see? You didn't think there was anything to understand about stuck bolts!

Dear Roger,

I really enjoyed your *Old Tractors* book and hope for a lot of sales for it. I want to add a bit of sympathy to your rusty bolts problem and offer a few notes about my experiences re: same. As an old farmer, engineer, gunsmith, mechanic, and machinist (master of none?), I also have had more run-ins with rusted fasteners than my blood pressure should deserve.

Any bolt or nut is in TENSION when installed, and rusts tightly against the LOOSEN direction of its threads where the metal to metal fit is the tightest. All threads have some clearance (class of fit) and if you can move the bolt or nut in the TIGHTEN direction a very small amount first off, things get a lot better quickly. This holds true of the stub even if the bolt has twisted off.

IDEAS:

A good sharp impact straight inward on the bolt with heavy hammer and short, solid punch. On a nut, use hammer and smaller socket wrench. [You] can hold a ball-peen hammer against bolt and hit the rounded end with a heavy hammer.

This helps direct the blow and prevents distorting the bolt. Wear safety glasses; hammers aren't supposed to hit each other. Repeat the heavy blows, try turning, repeat, try doing both together simultaneously. That's the magic of a good air-impact wrench—get one, firstest!! But first hammer the thing anyway. You'll feel better for it if nothing else. Air wrenches can't "feel" that "oh-oh" stage.

If no luck, try heat—acetylene torch best—on bolt, then wallop it a few licks as above when good and hot. Not real hot—too soft then. Let it cool to shrink down, then try wrench. Repeat a few times. The heat/cool expansion/contraction cycles and the inward impacts work wonders.

Still no luck? While pretty warm, touch paraffin wax on joint and let it melt and flow into threads. It flows very well if pretty hot and works much better than any oil I've tried. Try more impacts now.

No? Maybe drilling is next, but try to drill clear through the bolt with a small bit, and then heat/apply paraffin into hole to soak from the back side. More clearance around threads from there. Then hammer, twist, and pray—to atone for the cursing sure to have come by this point.

Prayers not answered? Now try some patience. Heat/cool/lube/ twist/rest/wait. If you're working with a stud, by all means try an EZ-Out *but* by all means get the ones with the bottoming-out shoulder on 'em. Hit 'em on the end as you twist; the other kind just swell the bolt in tighter often. Still stuck? Personally I then suggest bourbon myself, amount being a personal matter. Tomorrow I try again. Good luck.

—Carl W. Andersen

I keep a bottle of good single-malt scotch in my shop. When someone points at it, conspicuous among all the automotive stuff, I explain, "Solvent." Closer to truth than you might imagine. Isn't that great stuff from Carl?

DAY 9

Bolt Breaker, First-Class

I SUPPOSE I SHOULD CELEBRATE the lovely weather— gorgeous for mid-December, but the fact of the matter is, balmy days like this are best spent doing outside work. (Today I stack firewood, prune trees in the lane that broke the rearview mirrors off my pick-up truck last fall, clean the patio.) So, as usual, the work in the office and playtime in the shop get lost. I do however find a couple spare hours late this afternoon. I continue scraping and cleaning Woodpecker.

Because of the broken oil fitting, and because I'm going to have to clean that engine block really well to re-insert the sleeves, and because there are only four bolts holding that engine to the transmission, I decide to pull the engine—or what's left of it, since without any fittings, manifolds, water pump, head, pistons, cylinders, or oil pan, there's really not much there—off the tractor.

This is complicated a little by the fact that both my engine stands are already loaded with engines. My thought was that I might have time this winter to work on a couple spare engines, so I took two engines off of parts tractors and put them on stands so I could move them around the shop as needed and work on them later. (I have this dream of fixing an engine up to perfection and mounting it on wheels so I can use it as a test unit; if I know everything on the tractor works well, then I can mount a questionable carburetor on it and give it a spin, knowing that problems that show up are likely to be *carburetor* problems.) Well, now I need a stand, so I'll have to use my engine hoists to lift an engine off a stand, set it on block on the floor, and then lift the engine (I know I said in *Old Tractors and the Men Who Love Them* that tractor engines are called "motors" but it's a hard habit to break) out of Woodpecker and put *it* on the stand so I can turn it over and work on it comfortably.

That involves a lot of pushing, shoving, prying, and juggling, and since everything is heavy, it can be dangerous. Since The Woodpecker is already in a state of dismantlement (is there such a word in the world outside of tractor work, I wonder?), I decide to loosen, maybe even remove one of the side rails holding the tractor together. That would open up one entire side of the engine and make the job of removing it a lot easier. I've done this before by simply loosening the side bolts and prying the side rail out far enough to let the engine slip out. I'll start with that plan.

I loosen the bolts holding the rail, except for one fastening the rail to the front steering pedestal. While all the other bolts come loose without trouble this one seems a little on the firm side. I tug at the breaker bar. Still stuck. I pull a little harder . . . and . . . it moves loose. It's still a little stiff but it is turning and . . . plink. Jeez, it wasn't turning at all. I was twisting the bolt and now I've broken it off, below the level of the rail, inside the cast-iron pedestal. Suddenly what was a minor job has become a major project, just like that. Now the rail has to come off and the broken bolt has to come out, but that can wait until after I pull the engine. For the moment I just spread the rails a bit with a handyman jack.

I have a little trouble shoe-horning the block around the steering shaft, because I imagine the ideal is to take the steering shaft off first and then lift out the block, but the steering knuckle is so rusty and worn and the pins holding it to the shaft is . . . well, I can't even tell what they are any

more—maybe old bolts that had the tar pounded out of them somewhere along the line so now they're nothing more than blobs of mutilated steel.

With the block out of the way, it's no problem getting a four-inch grinder to the steering knuckle and grinding both ends of the pins flush with the knuckle. Then I douse them with penetrating oil, put a straight punch to them, and knock them right out. Once the pins are out, the knuckle slides right off.

At this point, there's not much left of the tractor on the two frame rails—the rear end, two rear wheels, the front pedestal, the transmission from the clutch case back, and the seat. Linda comes in to tell me supper will be about another hour, commenting that the old Woodpecker looks for all the world like an oversized skateboard. She's right, too.

Still flushed with victory, I spend a little time putting new fittings on the business end of my air hose and go in for supper, feeling as if I'm getting closer every day to being a first-class mechanic.

| Day 9 hours: | 2.0 |
| Total project hours | 33.0 |

Little Victories

IT'S ALREADY MID-AFTERNOON SO I DON'T have a lot of time for the shop today, but I haven't been out here except to check on my hams and throw a piece or two of wood in the stove during the past week, so I feel I'm overdue. I like to start these days cleaning things up, putting away tools, generally re-assessing where I am on this project. I scrape off a little more dirt and grease. I look at that broken oil fitting on the engine again. I peer inside the clutch housing and assess problems there.

I've known for the past couple weeks that somehow I pulled the tractor a little too far into the shop. I have plenty of room behind it, where I really don't need room, but not nearly enough up front, where I'm going to need to get an engine hoist in to lift the front end and transmission off the frame rails. I'm not tickled about having to jack the tractor up and off the jack stands, back it up a couple feet, jack it back up and set it back on the stands, but . . . I do it.

It's not much of a problem jacking it up and taking away the stands. There is a problem, however, in moving the tractor back. As I have mentioned, I put some old steel wheels without lugs on the back, just to narrow up the wheel base and make it easier to roll the tractor into the shop. And I put some old iron wheels on the front too, simply to make the tractor roll-able. The tractor is a lot lighter by now, if you think of all the parts I have taken off this thing, but still, I have trouble getting the darned thing to roll. For one thing, I've taken off so many parts, there's not much left to push on!

I often move my working tractors a few inches forward or back not by pushing on the body but by applying pressure to the large back wheels where I can get some leverage. Maybe that will work here too. If not, maybe I can get a lever of some kind on that big back wheel and turn the tractor back those few inches I need. I have managed to break loose the rusted clutch lever and disengage the clutch, and the brakes are free. There are bolt heads on the rear wheels which may give me some trouble in rolling the tractor back, but I should be able to muscle that. The wheels seemed to move easily enough when I had the machine up on jack stands. Yet the tractor does not seem happy about moving. I can rock it, but it won't roll.

I rock the tractor trying to get it rolling backward. I hear a funny clanking, whirring sound behind me. I turn to see that the belt pulley is also turning. The belt pulley is a big drum coming directly off the transmission, used to drive other equipment with a wide, long leather or cloth belt. I use the belt pulley on Sweet Allis to turn the buzz saw with which I cut the very firewood burning in my stove.

Hmmm. If the belt pulley turns when I rock the wheels . . . maybe the wheels will turn when I spin the belt pulley! Now, if you're an old-timer, you're probably thinking I'm a damned idiot not to know such a thing, but I've admitted frequently in these pages that I *know* I'm an innocent in such matters, and that that's what I love so much about it—discovery and learning! So, I step back and easily turn the belt pulley a couple times . . . the back wheels turn evenly, rolling the tractor easily back where I want it, just like that! Wow.

It's been a short shop-day, only two hours, but the victories this time have been unexpected and fun. Maybe I should have included that with the reasons for pursuing this goofy business of old tractor restoration: discovery, learning, and little triumphs.

Day 10 hours:	2.0
Total project hours	35.0

Differential Strokes

I SHOULD SPEND THE ENTIRE DAY working in the shop with the big doors open, it's so pretty for December, but my parents are coming out to visit us in a couple days and I better have everything shipshape in the shop or my Old Man will let me know that I wasn't raised this way. So I empty the trash buckets, sweep the floor, tidy up, put away tools, close drawers, hang up cords, chains, and wires, mop up spills and spots. I put together some new shelving for the shop library—the most important factor, to my mind, of a good shop. I empty the coffee cans I've had sitting under the final drive drain plugs, collecting the filthy oil, grease, and water from them. I wonder if they've been drained since this machine was put together in West Allis, Wisconsin, 60 years ago? I pull a drain pan—okay, a plastic laundry tub—under the differential so I can drain that component too, but find it won't be all that easy.

First, the rear end is caked with dirt and grease, which apparently had been protected by the old corn picker. I can't even find the drain plug under it. I squirt solvent (mineral spirits, in this case) on the dirt to soften it up. Then I scrape and push at it. It is the consistency and color of well-aged road tar. I finally have to get an old wood chisel and light hammer to pound some of the caked stuff off. I finally get down to the plug and use one of my dental tools to clean out the square hole so I can insert a ⅜-inch drive and turn it out.

Whoa! That's not going to be all that easy either: The differential clearly has been drained before, and whoever did it, had some trouble getting the plug out. The marks are unmistakable: the "mechanic" in this case pounded at the plug with hammer—not unusual—and *chisel!* . . .

putting three deep gashes in the plug, and in the process pretty well mucking up the recess where I intended to insert the ratchet. So, I get out my chisel and a light hammer and tap away at the plug. It comes loose with surprising ease, finally turning out by hand. So why did Bozo Number One mess up the plug for Bozo Number Two if the plug wasn't stuck? Who knows.

Another pleasure in my fuddy-duddy life is crossword puzzles. Linda is mystified by the process, but I explain to her that it's not just me filling in little squares with letters. (My son Chris once helped me out with a particularly tough puzzle by saying, "Jeez, Dad, just stick in a bunch of Ms and Os!") In my mind it's a contest of wit between me and the person who built the puzzle in the first place. He or she is trying to baffle me, confuse me, out-think me, and I try to overcome the process.

There's some of that in this old tractor business. It's not simply a matter of me against cold, hard, rusted iron. I like to think I can outwit a brass nut, most of the time anyway. The contest is between me and the engineer who designed the tractor against whatever the problem was he or she faced 60 years ago and I face now. Then it comes down even more specifically to me trying to think like the dolt who mucked up the job of repairing the problem the last time. The paradigm goes something like this: a water pump jacket broke on some farmer's Allis WC one day when he was out trying to pick corn. He probably knew what he should have done to fix it right, but there was this storm gathering on the horizon, he was already late with the har-

vest, he didn't have the money to buy a new pump, and he figured he would do what he could right out in the field, and take care of the problem correctly during the winter when he had more time and money.

So he goobers up the pump with some road tar and holds it together with some baling wire and a good piece of egg box wood. During the winter he thinks about the problem a couple of times but never remembers to get the thing repaired. Once when he's in town he goes to the new Allis dealer to get a new pump, but while he's there he looks at the new Allis WD and figures why spend money on a pump when what he really needs is a new tractor. So he buys a new tractor, hauls the old WC out to the wood lot and parks it in the elms. I get it 30 years later . . . and the pump is still messed up. Now it's up to me to figure out not only how a water pump works but also how to get around the mess this guy has made of the one on this tractor.

Bozo One + Bozo Two + Bozo Three = potential solution to mechanical problem.

Nothing comes out of the differential, not even water. Hmmm. Empty? Maybe. I get a long, thin-bladed filleting knife and poke around in the hole, jab, probe, scrape . . . and . . . HERE IT COMES! Great gobs of filthy black grease glug out, with distressing signs of metal flakes mixed in. Eventually I'll rinse out the rear end with kerosene so I can get a better look at what's going on in there. When I turn the wheels, there aren't any disturbing clunks or grinding, so . . . we'll have to see.

Before I close everything up for the evening, I go around what's left of the tractor and the engine with a can of penetrating oil, squirting it liberally on rusty bolts and stuck fittings. It's truly amazing how the stuff can work over the period of a couple hours, and miraculous what it can do over a week's time.

Day 11 hours	1.0
Total project hours	36.0

🚜 *DAY 12* 🚜

Crank Problems

WELSCH WEATHER REPORT

Still unseasonably warm.

THERE'S SOMETHING COMFORTING about the warmth of a shop from which you can look out on blowing snow, but then again, the more I think of it, there's something comforting about the warmth of a shop when the weather is good, too. Today I spend time yet once again cleaning up and putting away tools, stowing cans and rags, and packaging plastic bread bags I use for trash and cleaned parts.

I jack up the tractor again and rechock it so I can get the wheels free and off; the back wheels are sitting cockeyed on their lugs and need to be taken off, the threads dressed on the lugs, and put back on more carefully. I need to get the front end off the blocks so I can check the seals and bearings in the vertical steering pedestal. I am pleasantly surprised to find that the front end is really pretty tight. Again, despite the generally disreputable condition of ol' Woodpecker, her innards may be in better shape than I anticipated . . . and feared. [Author's note: Jeez, more hubris. Won't this guy ever learn?! Every time I talk about how great things are going and how easy this is going to be, I ensure that something is going to go wrong sooner or later. Probably sooner. And maybe later too.]

I take off the metal lid covering the top access port of the front end to inspect the steering mechanism. The gears all seem clean and tight, probably in part because there is a sound gasket under the lid, the first I have seen in the couple dozen Allis WC front ends I've opened up. But whoops . . . what's this?! As I turn the crank extension that runs from the front of the tractor back to the socket on the crankshaft, I note that it seems to catch a little. Then it turns freely . . . and catches again. As I roll the extension, I can see it is bent, and as the convex part of the bend rolls under . . . it hits the top of the steering vector (the big partial gear that turns the front wheels). The crank extension is going to have to come out of the front pedestal and be straightened.

I look the crank extension over, and like so much on these old girls, it doesn't seem all that complicated. There is a pin on the rear of the extension that catches on the socket mounted to the front of the crankshaft when the engine is started, and there is a pin on the very front that fits into the hand crank. I squirt the pins with penetrating oil and bang on them a little with a hammer. The front pin seems a little loose. With a grinder, I take off the burr on both ends of both pins and, with a punch, bang on them. The back one almost falls out; the front pin (which needs to be replaced anyway because one end has worn off) takes a little more time and work but it too comes out cleanly. I pull out the crank extension and roll it on the cement floor; the bend is clearly visible. I probably shouldn't get too cocky [Author's note: !!!] but I don't think straightening it is going to be that much of a job. I might be able to do it with a couple taps of a hammer—if not, with a couple cranks of the shop press.

I fill the differential and final drives with kerosene to clean them out. It never fails to surprise me how well kerosene cuts heavy grease and oil. I clean up the spills and spatters on the floor, also with kerosene. I hate to leave spills and spots on my shop floor because I'll be tracking the stuff all over if I don't get at it right away. I dump the waste oil from the differential and final drives in my waste-oil barrel outside the shop. One of these days I'd love to find a heating stove that burns waste oil. Is there such a thing, I wonder?

The throttle base mounted on the steering-wheel stand is in pretty bad shape. All the little cogs that are supposed to hold the throttle arm in place are badly chewed up, and someone goobered it up with blobs of welding rod so it would still work, sort of. I take it off too in case I can do something with it later on. I have plenty of spares, so I may just replace it with one in better shape.

Lots of little victories today. Not much left on the frame of Woodpecker. I wonder how she feels about being this naked.

Day 12 hours	2.0
Total project hours	38.0

Goo Removal

**WELSCH
WEATHER
REPORT**

It's just about Christmas yet the temperature is nearly 60 degrees. Not the sort of thing we expect in Nebraska every year.

TODAY I WORK WITH THE SHOP doors open. I probably should practice my welding because I wouldn't have to put up with all the smoke and smell, but I get started instead cleaning up the tools from yesterday's work. A lot of mechanics prefer to clean up right away at the end of the day, but I like to use the process as the start of my time in the shop. The ritual of cleaning and putting away the tools helps me remember where I am in the job and to think about what's to be done next.

I pour kerosene into the transmission and roll the gears to clean them up. I love the way the ages of grease and dirt wash off the iron. I can't help but think how good it must feel to be an old, nearly-dead tractor, suddenly being renewed and cleaned up, cared about and loved. Maybe that's because I'm old and nearly dead myself! The reverse gear at the bottom of the transmission case is sticky on the shaft it is supposed to slide on, but in the kerosene bath it quickly breaks loose and begins to move smoothly. What a great feeling!

I hear a little drip below me. I'm not surprised. Sometimes it's only the dirt and rust that is holding these things together. When you take off the dirt and rust, well . . . As I scrape at the grease and dirt on the outside of the power take-off case at the bottom of the transmission, kerosene almost fountains out. Bad seal, maybe bad bearing, I'd guess. Well, it's another job, but as I have to remind myself too, replacing that seal and bearing will be another challenging, maybe even fun day in the shop. Woodpecker will be grateful, I know. I shove a plastic tub under the transmission to catch the dripping kerosene from the PTO housing during the night. (The next day when I check on things in the shop, the transmission and PTO are empty, all the kerosene having leaked out. The seal must be completely gone.)

While I'm cleaning the inside of the transmission, I also scrape away at the outside. Once the worst of the dirt and grease is off, I paint it liberally with kerosene to loosen the most stubborn of the goo. Tonight it can drip into the tub under the transmission too.

I open the brake boxes over the final drives. They look pretty clean but I'll pay more attention to them later, probably rinsing them with kerosene, too. I scrape a little on the outside and inside of the steering pedestal. One of my ambitions is to haul a tractor into my shop to work on some day and take the time to bring a couple big plastic garbage cans into the shop. I'll label one "iron" and the other "dirt" and then in one I'll put every piece of old iron—baling wire, bent nails, old bolts, useless scraps, hair pins and safety pins—and in the other I'll put every bit of dirt I scrape off. I'll bet I would wind up with a couple hundred pounds of both.

Because the weather is so nice, I haul the corn picker fans out of the shop and stow them in a shed. It'll be a good year before I can do anything about them so there's no sense in having them in the way. While I'm outside, I look around at some other engine blocks. I'm beginning to think I'll want to replace the block on The Woodpecker. Of course I won't throw the old one away. You never know when you might need a block, even with a broken off oil fitting stuck in it and a crack running from stem to stern.

Day's done—three glorious hours. I wish I had three hours like this every day.

Day 13 hours:	3.0
Total project hours	41.0

The Mystery
of Needle Bearings

SOMEHOW I MANAGED TO PUT THE drain tub under
the transmission slightly out of kilter, so I find a gal-
lon of kerosene spread on the floor. I spend more
than an hour I should have been working on The
Woodpecker cleaning the floor instead. Not too
mention that it's cold. In a way that's okay: I am a little uneasy about where things are going with The
Woodpecker.

Dan the Plumber comes by this morning and
assesses my progress. I'm never sure if my buddies,
who are each and everyone a mechanic of some
accomplishment, come to laugh at me or what, but they always help me
out (with my beer supply if not always my restoration problems).

"Listen to this," I say, turning the drive shaft by hand. "Hear that funny
little tinkling sound? Bearings?"

He puts his ear to the front end of the transmission case where it enters
the clutch housing. "Bearings."

"But they sound loose, like they're banging up against each other."

"Needle bearings," he says. "No cage, just little rods rolling around
loose around the shaft."

"Man, that sounds like nothing but trouble to me. How does one re-
insert loose little rollers around a shaft and then insert it into a case? I
can't imagine."

Dan has confirmed my worst suspicions: There are such things as needle bearings. How the heck do you put those loose little cylinders back
into their place? I have tried a couple times, but it seems absolutely
impossible. "Thick grease," is Dan's answer. On several occasions I have

taken apart components and found loose cylindrical bearings with no signs of a cage to hold them. I couldn't hardly believe it, but it seemed unlikely that the cage had just worn away or shattered.

It's been a couple years since I dismantled my parts tractor completely (the tractors I have since "parted out" I have left in component lumps) so I don't recall what things look like inside that wall between the transmission and clutch housing. I therefore haul in the worst transmission I have in my parts inventory and tear into it, a filthy job. When I finally get into the location I am concerned about . . . there it is . . . or rather, there they are: 17 little rollers—or at least what may have once been rollers, because they are now worn into triangular slivers, even in this parts tractor. I guess that particular component must be a fairly frequent casualty.

That means the likelihood of finding replacement bearings in another of my parts transmissions are slim. I'll try to find new ones at the Allis dealership down the road about 30 miles. They won't be cheap, and I'm not going to dismantle the clutch housing on Woodpecker until I find out if I can get new bearings and seals. If I can't get new ones, well, I may just have to pack the loose ones in The Woodpecker with heavy grease and let them go. After all, The Woodpecker may never run more than a couple hours a year for the rest of her life. She'll run four or five hours at her champagne reception, I'll start her a little every spring and fall, and that may be about it. Faulty clutch shaft bearings won't make much of a difference with an easy retirement life like that. But one of the surprising things I've found in my old tractor work is that parts are still available for tractors that haven't been manufactured for better than 50 years. I can't imagine why, but they are.

Tonight before I go to sleep I'll spend some time reading my shop manuals and thinking about how exactly to attack that bearing problem. Beats worrying about Muslim militants or the war in Bosnia. After all, there is a real chance I can do something about the bearings!

Day 14 hours:	2.0
Total project hours	43.0

Making Parts

I've rarely seen so much practical advice in a one-page letter as the following from Doit Ross of Minooka, Illinois. Three great ideas—and one curious mystery I don't want to know anything more about.

Roger,

My wife bought your book for me for Christmas and I enjoyed it very much. Being an old tractor nut also, I thought that I would pass on a couple of helpful hints I never have seen published:

1. To make gaskets for small parts, run the old one, or the piece, over the library duplicator and super glue the picture to the gasket material. (It helps to have an accomplice divert the librarian.)

2. Buy the biggest army surplus ammo box you can find, fill it ¼ full of diesel fuel, put your small parts, bolts, nuts, etc. in it. Put it in the back of your parts-chasing vehicle. By the time you get your parts rounded up, the stuff you already have will be sparkling clean.

3. To remake "plastic" parts, repair the old one with Bondo, super glue, or anything else that will work, spray it with cooking oil, put RTV-silicone caulk in a paper cup and press in the piece. Let this set up, then remove the part. You now have a rubber mold. Mix two-tube epoxy and fill mold. Eureka! A new piece.

4. One word of advice: Don't buy a sawmill.

—Doit Ross

Busted Knuckles

WELSCH WEATHER REPORT

Pea-soup foggy, a good day to be in the shop because it's so quiet, because I am coming off several days of frustrating imprisonment in my office, and because I am facing a few days of work with a television crew. I decide, therefore, to spend all day in the shop by way of preemptive therapy.

THE VERY FIRST THING I DO, OF COURSE, is spill a quart of filthy kerosene on the floor. It takes me a half hour to clean it up. Then I dump the plastic bucket I keep all my washers in on the floor. Without the slightest notion how or when, I apparently hurt my finger, because the nail is now turning deep black. All day long I nick myself, squeeze flesh into blood blisters, drop tools and parts, burn myself, and drip blood. It's not unusual for me to get a bruise or cut during a shop day, but today is nothing but self-inflicted damage. I have no idea why but there's not much question that my karma is in bad shape today.

I try turning the big bolts holding on the side rail again, however, and—aha! They come loose. All that juicing and tapping is paying off. I remove the heavy side rail and gain access to the broken bolt in the front end. I put a stout support under the transmission, since now there is nothing left of The Woodpecker but one side rail, the rear drive, the front end, and the transmission (supported only on one side). I clean off and remove the leaky PTO transmission (and again, dirty kerosene drains all over my floor).

Dan Selden comes drifting through—it's a Saturday, so he's off work—and looks things over. He listens to the loose bearings between the clutch and transmission housing and urges me to 1) forget it, considering how little work ol' Woodpecker will ever be expected to do the rest of its life, or 2) simply drop in one of my spare transmissions, whole.

Well, the second option isn't attractive because there's every possibility that every other used transmission I have needs bearings too. Every one I have dismantled thus far—about 10—has. The first option is probably the wisest one, or would be if I were a real mechanic, or a real farmer. But I'm not. I'm a hobbyist. I am doing this, I remind myself yet once again, for fun. Part of the fun—if I can find new bearings and they are not prohibitively expensive—will be repairing this very real problem. I decide to leave the clutch housing together until I hear from Wayne Hilder over at the Deutz-Allis dealership in Central City about what he's found out about the clutch housing drive shaft bearings.

In the meanwhile, I haul a spare engine into the shop and dismantle it. Believe me, the process of taking apart an engine on a stand where you can move all around it is altogether different from trying to take one apart while it is still on the tractor! I drop the oil pan, pull the head, take off the water pump. Everything goes smoothly, except that the engine is full of mouse residue—nests, hair, seeds, nut hulls, and poop.

I turn the engine over on the stand, marking the four rods and rod caps with metal stamps so I could be sure to keep the same caps with the same rods and put them back into the engine with the same orientation. The process is simply a matter of putting a stamp against the metal and tapping it with a light hammer. Worth the trouble when the time comes to put this all back together, believe me. I push the four pistons out the top of the block and they come out relative easily. They are clean, most of the rings free and loose. The encouraging discovery is welcome, especially in light of the condition of my poor battered body by the time my first hour in the shop is over.

The crankshaft should rotate totally freely now, since hardly anything is still attached to it, but it seems to catch now and then. I peer inside the case of the timing gear and the whole things is stuffed full of the same damned mice junk the rest of the engine has suffered. The nutshells, weed seeds, and droppings are jamming up in the gears. This would be the perfect time to have a shop vacuum.

In fact, a shop vacuum like the one Lovely Linda bought me for Christmas. Unfortunately, that machine, which looks quite a bit like R2D2 from "Star Wars," had about 1,200 horsepower and tended to suck in the windows whenever I turned it on, so I took it back. I didn't get one better adapted for my modest needs. So I am confined to blowing the dirt out with my compressor hose, pretty much filling the whole shop with stinky mouse dirt. Terrific. I'll probably die of a new disease—Welsch's Mouse Dirt Syndrome.

When I've gotten the light stuff out, I flush the block with kerosene, spilling another quart of filthy stuff on my floor. By this time my language has turned real ugly, and it's just noon. After lunch, I get the crankshaft free and moving easily, and I only hurt myself three or four times in the process. What is going on with me?

Now I turn my attention back to The Woodpecker. Off and on I've tinkered at the broken bolt in the front end pedestal, one of the eight that holds the front end in the side rails, but it shows no signs of loosening. I decide to get serious. I drill a small hole right down the middle of it, all the way through it. I heat it to red hot and spray water down the hole with a syringe, hoping the contraction might break it loose. Nothing. I spray penetrant into the hole and decide to let it soak another week or two. I would rather not have to drill it out completely since this process has a high potential for messing up the threads in the front end, especially on a day like this when everything else seems to be going wrong. I tap it a couple times for good measure.

Finally, I face reality. Nothing is going to get better. I don't want to give up the last couple hours of this time I have reserved for the shop, so I take a couple of the pistons from the original engine over to my work bench, rinse them with kerosene to get the worst of the dirt off, and spend the rest of the afternoon carefully chipping off burnt-on carbon, fried grease, and oil. There's something comforting about the process of transforming a fairly ragged piece of iron into a shiny, nearly new one. Aside from the unpleasantness of dirty kerosene flowing over and into open wounds. (I've tried rubber gloves for such process but really don't like them, besides which, they always tear and then you have kerosene on your wounds even when you're *not* working in the stuff.)

Cleaning these things takes a while. I use a dental pick to scrape and chip the tough, black carbon from under the piston rings and then rinse each ring with clean kerosene. I gently rub the pistons' stained sides with a light, plastic scouring pad. Same with the rods, Babbitt bearings, and rod caps. I clean the ring groves with a piece of broken compression ring. I have a cleaner manufactured for the purpose but a broken ring is cheaper, more convenient, and easier on the soft metal of the piston.

I was once asked where the heck one gets a piece of broken compression ring to use for this purpose. I couldn't help but think of the old story that if you are ever cornered by a grizzly bear, stuff some human feces up his nose because they absolutely hate human feces. The standard reply to such advice is, "Where the heck would I find human feces in a situation like that?" to which the answer is, "Oh, just reach around behind you. It'll be there all right."

Same with compression rings. Work with engines a couple days and when you need a broken ring, oh, it'll be there all right.

It takes me about an hour and a half for each piston, so by the time I go in for supper, I've finished only two. That's okay. Despite all my injuries, the quiet process of cleaning parts has turned this into a good day and I feel that I've gotten something accomplished. The big problem for me at this point is still that broken bolt in the front end. I keep wishing one of these times I'll apply a little pressure on it and feel it give and turn out of that hole where it's been locked for almost 60 years now. One way or the other, one way or the other . . .

I've had six good hours in the shop today. Linda is mystified as I come in bloody and filthy, *whistling* a merry tune.

Day 15 hours:	6.0
Total project hours	49.0

Welding 101

WELSCH WEATHER REPORT

Another beautiful, warm day for January.

I'D LOVE TO WORK ON THE WOODPECKER but it's nice enough to open the doors to the shop, so I decide to practice welding.

As usual, everyone in town has plenty of advice for me and my aspirations in the wild world of welding. Dan Selden answers my plea for information about how to avoid rods sticking in my work by bringing me a teflon rod. It's a regular 6012 welding rod wrapped with plumbers teflon joint tape. A sample of my welding I leave at the tavern in town winds up with the scribbled message and critique on it, "DO NOT DROP! FRAGILE!!" One helpful friend suggests that maybe I should practice for a while with cardboard and Elmers glue before graduating to welding rod and electricity, oxy-acetylene and brazing.

Also as usual, there are long recitations of pants cuffs catching on fire, globules of melted steel dropping precisely and painfully through the lace holes of boots only to burn through socks and skin and flesh of innocent welders. I've had bad dreams for months about tales of welding overhead seams, drops of white hot metal dropping into the welder's ear, certain to cause horrible damage...if there were anything in there to damage.

I do what I can to contribute to my own legends and the general body of welding tales. The very first time I strike an arc, I throw up my helmet and admire my very first weld—not at all bad, considering. Then I smell something funny, and learn that it's really important to pick up scraps of paper, rags, and cardboards from the floor and welding area before getting started. Actually, it's not all that bad: I get all the fires stomped out before anything really serious happens. And I check my shop fire extinguishers and make sure they are readily accessible and that I know where they are.

I suffer any number of minor burns...and one terrible one that takes

weeks to heal up. Curious how all my welder friends who have had so little to contribute to my knowledge of the craft have so much to say about the consequences of me not know what it is they might have told me! Bit by bit, I learn the importance of each and every item of protective gear, even long-sleeved shirts.

After one particularly intense day of working with the stick welder, I take some samples up to the tavern for evaluation by the experts but as usual they have little to say about the welds...a lot to say about the clear and intense redness growing across my lower arms as the radiation burn from the welding arc grows ever redder, ever more obviously painful. I roll down my shirt sleeves (better late than never) and Eric offers to turn down the lights in the tavern. I thank him, thinking he is perhaps being sympathetic to my embarrassment. No, I judge too fast. He explains that as much as I am glowing, he'll even give me a couple free beers if I just sit there glowing through the evening and light the place for him, cutting back on the electrical bill he is always complaining about.

The books all say that welding can be painful if you're not careful. They never mention exactly that the pain has more to do with ego, however, than ache.

As the day cools off, however, I spend the last hour and a half cleaning another piston, nice, quiet, dirty work.

An hour and a half in the shop today, but not much to show for it . . . except good feelings.

| Day 16 hours | 1.5 |
| Total project hours | 50.5 |

The Joy of Recycling

I WORKED ALL DAY IN THE OFFICE, so it really feels good to get into the shop, even if it is just another piston day.

Sometimes I worry about the state of my mind when I'm doing this. Why is it that I loathe washing dishes, but I absolutely love sitting out here in the shop washing parts with kerosene? It certainly isn't the smell or pain of kerosene soaking into scratches, cuts, and burns. I do admire clean, shiny parts all lined up, but the real secret, I think, is how they start—which is to say, filthy. I love the idea of these utterly disreputable items being transformed into something pretty.

I imagine it hearkens back to my primal inclination toward recycling. I bought our house for $350—an abandoned wreck, which we then rebuilt. I liked the idea of taking something discarded and making it into something useful. One of my children is adopted—a soul thrown away by one person, salvaged by us. My farm was a virtual throw-away, a waste-land made even less viable by over-grazing, misfarming, poor management on poor soil; we've rebuilt it into a natural paradise. I like taking old tractors, junk to others, and making them run and live again. I guess that curious inclination on my part goes right down to old pistons and oil pumps too.

| Day 17 hours | 1.5 |
| Total project hours | 52.0 |

Welding 102

WELSCH WEATHER REPORT

Cold but clear.

AGAIN, I WIND UP WITH ONLY AN hour of spare time at the end of a long, frustrating day. I *have* to get a full day out here some time soon. It's not so much a matter of getting more done on The Woodpecker as saving my sanity.

I'm still banging at that stuck, broken bolt in the front end pedestal casting. There is still no movement to it. Next step is to weld a nut on it and try to turn it out that way. Big step for me. A *real* welding job! My first one.

In the short time I have for the shop today I try out my carbon arc torch, using it to heat the broken and stuck brass fitting in The Woodpecker's old engine block. And it works. The torch fires up just fine, heats up the brass fitting, and then it turns right out. Wow. It sure is nice to have something go right for a change.

Okay, so then I start cleaning up the new block, since I am still wrestling with whether I will weld and use the old block or drop in a replacement. Even if I don't use this replacement engine, I'll put it into shape simply to have in my parts inventory.

I have the pistons out—those are the ones I'm cleaning—and the pan and head off. Now all I have to do is pull the sleeves and clean them up, re-insert them with new O-rings, generally clean up the block, and put the engine back together. Yeah, sure. I decide that since I don't have time to start pulling sleeves, I'll do the easy work and just spend a little time cleaning the block up. I scrape, steel-brush, squirt a little solvent here and there . . . and . . . and . . . and twist off the same damned oil fitting I busted off in Woodpecker. Terrific. Well, maybe I'll have the same kind of luck with the arc torch. I'll save that project for the next welding day. Meanwhile, I'll just keep cleaning the block.

Hmmm. What's this? Under this grease and dirt, there's . . . there's . . . there's a split. Jeez, this block is as bad as the one I took out of Woodpecker. And now it has a broken oil fitting stuck in it too. The Woodpecker doesn't. So just that fast, what was the worst block has become the best block and what was the best block has become the worst block. The moral of the story is, don't throw anything away just because it's the worst whatever at the moment. Tomorrow it may be the best whatever you have. If you've wondered why I've been wasting your time talking about working on a spare engine that really isn't a part of The Woodpecker, well, at this point it's hard to tell what is going to be a part of Woodpecker and what isn't.

Day 18 hours	1.0
Total project hours	53.0

The Joy of Grease

WELSCH WEATHER REPORT

Whew. Yet another beautiful day. This weather sure makes it hard to do real work in the office!

TODAY I HAVE A FULL AFTERNOON in the shop, a total of four hours. I'll come back into the house as the sun sets, having accomplished . . . absolutely nothing.

I spend the first two hours working at that miserable bolt broken off in the steering pedestal casting. I drill the hole down the center a little larger and try a bigger EZ-Out. Nothing. I bang on it. I heat it with propane. Nothing. I heat it and shoot cold water into its center with a hypodermic syringe. Nothing. I heat it with a carbon arc torch—gingerly, I might add, because I'm afraid I might wind up simply welding the bolt into its hole. Nothing. I bore the hole even larger, go through the heating processes again, try the biggest of my EZ-Outs. Nothing, nothing, nothing. Zip zero nada rien nichts nothing.

So I turn my attention to the replacement block I've been thinking of putting into The Woodpecker. I clean on it, scraping, scrubbing, squirting, and it is looking a lot better. Then I decide to pull the sleeves so I can install new O-rings and clean things up inside the block. Again I run smack into a brick wall. I tapped, squirted, and turned my sleeve puller down as hard as I could with every muscle in my fairly substantial body. Nothing. I finally take out the crankshaft so I can get at the bottom of the sleeves more easily. Another couple steps backward in the process.

Thing is, I am getting close to that glorious moment when I will turn the biggest corner there is in rebuilding a tractor, and I'm getting excited to get there: The moment will come, you see, when I will be finished taking things apart and can begin putting them back together. Another champagne evening. As close as I am to that moment, within sight of turning that corner, the bad drive shaft bearings, the broken bolt, and the

stuck sleeves form a barrier in front of me the size of Mt. Everest. So, I tell myself, "Self, you're doing this for fun. Don't forget that. Just think about what you're learning about shelled out bearings, broken bolts, and stuck sleeves! Hey, buddy, ain't you lucky?!"

And that's not all horse pucky, you know. If getting this machine going takes me two years, so what? The party up at Eric's will simply be all the more triumphant. In the meantime, I have to think like a doctor—not of the horrors I am finding in this poor, wracked body on the operating table in front of me, but of the good things I am doing to it, how much better it will feel when I'm finished. And, how much better I will feel!

When I come into the house tonight, drenched in dirt, grease, and sweat, Linda looks at me in horror. "Are you all right?" she asks.

"Gosh, yes, I'm fine," I grin. "In fact, damn fine." She shakes her head in disbelief.

"Don't forget," I laugh, as much for me as for her. "I'm doing this for fun!"

| Day 19 hours | 4.0 |
| Total project hours | 57.0 |

Bad Parts

WELSCH WEATHER REPORT

This has to be the most unusual Nebraska winter of the 58 I have endured—day after day of warm, balmy, sunlit skies. Today I work with the shop doors open even though it is February.

AGAIN I TRY THE SLEEVES OF THE replacement engine I am thinking of dropping into The Woodpecker. My problem is that two hurdles have stopped me dead in my tracks. First, there is that wretched broken bolt in the front end. I have drilled, heated, beat, turned, and drilled, heated, beat, and turned even more. There are no signs of capitulation on the part of the bolt. Or me. I will have to be extremely careful not to damage the threads inside the cast front-end housing but I suspect that what I will wind up doing, soon, is drilling as much of the bolt out as I can without hitting the threads in the front end and then use a dentist's pick to pry the little, wiry remains of that bolt out. It ain't gonna be a party, and I'm not looking forward to it.

Secondly, the drive shaft bearing in the wall between the clutch housing and transmission housing is still shot. (I once called my construction friend Mick Maun to complain that he had never replaced a window he had installed wrong. "WHAT?!" he sputtered in mock horror. "Is that window *still* broken?!") When I turn the shaft, I *still* hear the remains of that assembly tinkling around in there. No signs of spontaneous healing. My ever-faithful Allis dealer in Central City sends me a new set of bearings, and thank goodness, they weren't all that expensive—less than $10, so I suppose that too should be done pretty quick.

Moreover, they are not the dreaded "needle bearings" Dan Selden warned me direly and dourly about. They are simply roller bearings in a light cage. [Author's Note: as I will find out later in this case and others, it is not at all unusual once these roller bearings break up and start grinding around, sometimes for many years before anyone does anything about them, they chew up the cage metal into little splinters and bits, not at all recognizable as a bearing cage!] The process will be a matter of pulling off the clutch housing, removing the wrecked bearing, and installing the new. I know, I know. It won't be that easy.

The big problem for me is the situation with the engines. The engine that came with The Woodpecker is completely dismantled but has, it turns out, two bad splits along the block, and I ruined one of the pistons when I beat it out of the sleeve. The engine I had considered as a replacement also has a split block, but it's not as bad as the original. All four pistons are in good condition, but now I am having real trouble getting the old sleeves out. Even if I don't use this engine, those sleeves have to come out, though, so there's nothing to do but keep working at them. Having to retreat to a third engine or replacement block would constitute a real defeat and ego-buster, as far as I'm concerned. I'm not sure why, but I know it would.

However, there is some progress in that direction. Once I take out the crankshaft, I put the sleeve puller squarely on the sleeves and while I turn on the pressure, I hit the bottom plate of the puller, resting as it does against the bottom skirt of the sleeve, with a machinist's hammer. This breaks things loose. Thousandths of an inch by thousandths of an inch I now have two of the reluctant sleeves sneaking up over the top of the engine block. That's the secret—getting these things started. They've been sitting in that block without moving for 40 or 50 years, after all. They've been heated and cooled, caked in burned oil and dirt, hammered and sealed in place. Then they sat and rusted for another couple decades. Those are not the sort of processes and conditions encouraging easy movement of metal surface against metal surface!

One thing I have learned for sure on Woodpecker: If you are going to pull the sleeves or use a ridge reamer on them, do it while the engine is in the tractor and the blasted sleeves are still in the block! Otherwise the process is like wrestling two greased pigs at the same time. The block is now on a engine stand on wheels and every time I apply muscle and weight against the sleeve puller, I drag the engine stand all over the shop, from one end to the other, snarling and cussing all the way.

The bad news for the day is that in cleaning The Woodpecker's PTO case, I find that under the dirt and grease it is completely shot. The PTO is at the very bottom of the transmission housing on these tractors, so as water condenses, falls, and runs into the transmission through the cracked or missing rubber boot around the shift lever, it settles right to the bottom of that PTO box. It freezes, and the case breaks, every time. In this case, the entire bottom of the casting has broken out and is just hanging there by rust and side pressure. I suppose it could be welded, but I have several spare PTO units I've taken off other tractors, so I think I'll just use the parts from this one for spares and put another unit on. No big deal.

Six good hours in the shop but only four on Woodpecker. I think I'm coming down with a cold. It may be a while before I come out this way again. As you can see, I've been spending less than three and a half hours in each visit to my shop. Would I like to have a full eight hours in the shop? Well, yes, in my dreams. But I have some "real" work to do almost every day I wake up, and during the winter, even as pleasant as this one has been, it takes a little while to warm the shop up, and, finally, as tired as I am after four hours of hard work in the shop, I'm not sure I'm up to eight. Probably, when I get to the point where I'm doing more cleaning and putting together cleaned parts, the work won't be as hard as it has been in separating these old, rusty, battered parts.

Of course then it will be spring and I'll probably have even less time for the shop. So it goes, so it goes. I have to keep in mind that all too soon it will be more than a 100 degrees in the shade, this being Nebraska, and I'll be closing the shop's doors and turning on the air conditioner, glad to crawl around on the cool concrete under Woodpecker!

Day 20 hours	6.0
Total project hours	63.0

The EZ-Out Myth

IT TAKES ME MOST OF THE MORNING to get the shop warm enough to work, so once again, I wind up with only a half day to work . . . er, play. I am determined to do something about that blasted stuck, broken bolt in the front end. I've got to make some progress there or everything else is going to start being irrelevant. So, ignoring the piles of stuff I need to put away and the dirty floor, I get right to work. Just in case I might have some luck, I try an EZ-Out in the bolt as she stands. No such luck. I drill the hole a little larger and try again. Nothing. I'm not surprised. I've never managed to get a broken bolt out with an E-Z Out. So why do I try? Well, there may be a first time.

Okay, this is the point where there is no more room for subtlety. The bolt is not going to turn out. It has to be drilled out. That means I will use the largest drill bit I can slide easily in and out of the casting holes, without binding in the threads. I really have to be careful not to damage the threads any more than necessary, or I'll have to re-tap the hole, drill a larger hole in the frame beam, and use a bigger bolt to remount the frame on the front end, maybe grinding down the new bolt head so it doesn't look altogether out of place . . . a mountain more of work and time.

Obviously, this is not a mistake I want to make. I don't want to damage those threads in the pedestal casting. A good part of my success in this matter will depend on how close I was to the center of the bolt the first time I drilled it . . . actually, how close I was when I tapped a divot into it with a punch before I drilled it. In fact, this is the single most important factor in drilling out a broken bolt.

So I use a drill bit smaller than I think will do the job, still hoping maybe the bolt will be shaken loose, and figuring that maybe this smaller bit will just skim the tops of the female threads in the casting close enough that I'll be able to fish out the wreckage of the bolt with no damage to the casting.

Sure enough, it works. I was close in centering my punch but not exactly. My hole was just enough off center that the bit nicks one edge of the female threads and I have enough of the old bolt metal coming loose that I can maybe get the mess out. I use a small chisel and light hammer to catch just a bit of the bolt that still protrudes from the casting and tap the thin remains of the bolt enough to start bending the threads out of their grooves and into the middle of the hole that used to be occupied by the troublesome bolt. All at once, the whole thing breaks loose. I catch the remaining bolt parts with needle-nose pliers and pull out the tatters of the bolt's threads. Man, I feel like Alexander the Great must have felt when he looked around and saw there was no more of the world to conquer!

I run a thread chase—a wonderful device that looks like a bolt with grooves and can be used to clean up messy female threads (there are also nut-like chases for male threads)—in and out of the hole a few times, encouraged by how firmly it fits in the hole. The threads seem to be in good shape. I rinse the hole out with a couple squirts of kerosene, clearing out metal filings and dirt. Then I run in one of the other, good bolts to see how the threads are holding, and it is firm as can be. Wow. All that time and care was worth it. No one looking at this tractor will ever know how much time and work went into that one bolt, but I will, and I'm the one who counts on this baby!

Day 21 hours	3.0
(Three of the toughest hours so far.)	
Total project hours	66.0

DAY 22

Good Intentions

MY INTENTION IN KEEPING THIS JOURNAL was to share with those who are considering restoring a tractor, roughly how a typical rebuilding process goes. I know when I started working with old tractors, it would have helped if I had simply had some idea what was in store for me. How long it would take—months? Years? The rest of my life? I am a little concerned, therefore, that this hasn't been a *typical* restoration, at least not in terms of the weather. I started this project in October, and at this writing, it is late February. The ground would normally be covered with snow. Typically, the shop stove should be running pretty much full time, the woodpile getting dangerously low. I should be champing at the bit to get the big doors of my shop open so I can sweep it out and maybe do some welding without asphyxiating myself in the process.

But this winter, the winter of 1994–1995, has been anything but typical. Instead of high temperatures in the 20s, lows below zero, we have been having day after day of temperatures in the 50s, 60s, even the 70s. The stove is cold, stuffed full of paper, gaskets, oily clothes I want to burn the first morning it's a little cool in the shop. If anything, I haven't been doing much welding because a leather apron is so hot at these temperatures.

So, I am wondering how typical this tractor work really is. I suppose when it comes right down to it, there isn't such a thing as "typical." When it comes to Nebraska weather, only the unusual is usual. If I make a mistake in this book, I would rather have it on the conservative side. I'd rather give the impression the work is harder and takes longer than usual rather than lead you down the primrose path of thinking it's easier and quicker. That's the way I think it's going. My work on The Woodpecker is going more slowly than it might during a colder winter because it is so easy to find things to do outdoors. In part, it's the cold and snow that make my shop so warm and comfortable, a haven from the elements, so I'm probably spending less time there than usual, getting less than the normal amount of work done, taking a longer time at the rebuilding than might be expected.

Today is another of those beautiful days. With my farm tractor (as opposed to my fun tractors) I haul the two engine blocks I am considering for the Woodpecker to our paved parking lot, drag the power washer out of the garage, and turn on the pressure. The warm sun quickly dries out the cleaned iron and I take them back to the shop. At last both blocks are completely dismantled, ready for careful, detailed cleaning, new O-rings, honed sleeves, new gaskets, that sort of thing. I sweep out the shop and practice some welding.

Day 22 hours	2.0
Total project hours	68.0

The Golden Moment
of Turn-Around

**WELSCH
WEATHER
REPORT**

Spring in winter,
continued . . .

FOR THE FIRST TIME IN A LONG TIME, I have two days
in a row when I can work on The Woodpecker, yesterday and today. I find myself cornered yet again: I
can no longer delay a decision on the possibly-dam-
aged bearing between the transmission case and
clutch housing. The engine is now completely dismantled, the broken
bolt is out of the front end, everything that can come off the tractor is off,
except the clutch housing, the front end, and the single side rail that
holds the three remaining elements together. Not much of a tractor.

I look at the transmission and turn the shaft a couple times. I can hear
loose bearings clinking around, but the shaft does turn freely. Again I
consider my dilemma. This machine will probably never again run more
than a few hours a year the rest of my life, maybe the rest of its life. It will
never again pull a plow or harrow, maybe not even a wagon load of wood.
I could probably forget replacing the bearing and no one would ever
notice, the tractor would show no sign of difficulty. I consider moving on.

On the other hand, why am I doing this? I'm doing it to put this tractor back into shape. It doesn't matter if it ever does anything. In fact, the
point of this process is not the tractor but me. I want to learn about tractors and mechanicking. I want to *re-build* this tractor. So, why not do it? If
nothing else, I should pull the transmission apart and take a look at those
bearings, right? That's what I decide to do.

Sure enough, when I pull the drive shaft from the transmission case, a
handful of loose bearings fall into the case and onto the floor. The bearings are completely shelled out. Yeah, the tractor probably would have
run forever without making further trouble, but . . . So, I clean gears, clean
and grease all the bearings, pack the new bearings with clean grease, and

ease everything back together. And everything does ease back together with remarkable smoothness. The smoothness of the process has nothing to do with me. It's a matter of good engineering, simple design, and good, solid parts. It makes me feel good just to handle this stuff.

I bolt the clutch housing back in place, and bolt it again to the side rail. I get that goofy feeling again of wondering how the old Woodpecker feels about having her innards clean and coated with new grease again. Okay, bolts and iron don't think and feel, but I can't help but wonder, especially now, with this machine I'm getting so fond of.

Lovely Linda comes in the door of the shop and reminds me that I promised to fire up the grill and toss on a couple steaks for supper. I had forgotten, so I welcome her gentle reminder. Time to clean up. I clean a mess of tools and put them away, I clean up my hands and arms, I sweep up the loose bearings. And somewhere along here, I realize that I reached . . . ta-da! . . . the GOLDEN MOMENT OF TURN-AROUND!!

For me, there are distinct highs in rebuilding an old tractor, and they fall into a distinct list of priorities for me. The greatest moment of all is WHEN THE TRACTOR STARTS AGAIN. Nothing beats that magic. The second greatest event in the process of rebuilding a tractor is the GOLDEN MOMENT OF TURN-AROUND, the remarkable instant when you finish taking things off the tractor, finish taking it apart, and begin to put it back together.

Wow.

I once dismantled and rebuilt an 1872 log house with some friends. We worked for weeks at the dirty task of taking that building apart and hauling the parts a hundred miles to my farm. Then there was the moment when we put two huge, walnut sill logs on their new foundation, and actually stacked an end log on them. That moment came at the end of a long, exhausting day, but as we stood there, realizing that now we were no longer taking down the house but putting it up again, we were overwhelmed. There is no comparable moment, for example, in writing a book. That night my friends and I were so filled with joy and pride, we slept on the ground *inside* those three logs—just three logs, one resting on the other two, but to us it was the beginnings of a new castle.

Same thing with a tractor engine. That MOMENT OF GOLDEN TURN-AROUND is a powerful milestone in the process. Number three in my listing is the moment you haul the tractor into the shop to start renewing it, number four is the moment you start to work on it, number five is the celebratory party when your friends and family share your

accomplishment, and number 6 is all the little unexpected pleasures that
come along in any restoration work on an old tractor—the strip of leather
found under the gas tank, the final extraction of the broken front-end bolt,
the eventual loosening and removal of the stuck sleeves, that sort of thing.

I stand there a moment and look at what remains of The Woodpecker
with a new perspective. Now the problems become something entirely different. Now it is no longer a problem of stuck parts coming unstuck but of
new or cleaned parts being inserted, applied, attached, considered. In many
ways, now the job is much more complicated. Getting things unstuck is
fairly straightforward (and in all honesty, there will still be some of that as
I dismantle small elements of the tractor like the air cleaner, carburetor, gas
filter bowl, magneto, oil pump, on and on). Now there will be a lot of long,
tedious hours cleaning parts, assessing their condition, cutting gaskets,
clearing battered threads, and trying to fit old, pitted, warped, worn parts
back in place on old, pitted, warped, worn parts, trying to save as much as
possible, replacing only what is absolutely necessary, not using parts that
will necessitate taking something apart again further down the line. All at
once, the entire task has changed, turned around. Whew. What a moment.

I'm glad we're doing steaks for supper. A celebration seems to be in order.

Day 23 hours	3.0
Total project hours	71.0
to the MOMENT OF GOLDEN	
TURN-AROUND	

The Systematic Approach to Tractor Restoration

The most incredible February day I have seen in my life—the temperature is in the 80s, a full 14 degrees over the previous record for the day. By mid afternoon, it's almost too hot to work in the shop! A great day to throw open the big doors on the shop and bask in the warm sun as I work on The Woodpecker. What a great day! A perfect day! What could possibly go wrong on a day like this?!

NOW, WHAT WAS THAT DEFINITION again of "hubris?" In fact, a good example of hubris is when some idiot announces, "I'm glad we're doing steaks for supper. A celebration seems to be in order after THE GOLDEN MOMENT OF TURN-AROUND."

I've been looking forward to today in the shop because the weather is good and I am eager to get started building up The Woodpecker again. As I look over the sorry iron remnants resting on jack stands—remember, there is nothing left of this tractor at this point but one side frame rail, the transmission, the steering pedestal, and the rear end, minus wheels—I notice that I haven't finished cleaning off the back end, a couple pieces of the transmission, and some greasy dirt on the front pedestal. I decide that I'll kick off this day with the cleaning jobs. Start with a clean slate, so to speak.

So I dig out the scrapers, brushes, rags, drop cloths, and kerosene and start cleaning on the rear end. As I pry off huge gobs of grease and dirt, I find one gob is particularly reluctant, on the bottom of the differential housing. In fact, there seems to be a piece of steel in the middle of the goo. Why, yes . . . there are three holes where mounting bolts for the corn picker apparently went, and there should be a fourth to complete the square right *here*, where the lump is. Ah Jeez, it's another broken bolt!

Well, maybe I'll be lucky and it'll come off easily. I apply Vise-grip pliers. It doesn't budge. And I find myself once again in the tedious, painful process of squirting the stub with penetrant, hitting it with a hammer, trying to turn it out, squirting, hitting, prying, squirting, hitting, prying. Nothing, nothing, nothing . . . you remember the litany.

The rest of the day I clean off the transmission, scrape the old, petrified gaskets from it, and worry about that damned broken bolt in the rear end. All day long I keep crawling back under the back end, squirting, banging, twisting, dreading the thought that once again I'm going to have to drill, heat, cool, drill, heat, cool—all those tortuous tasks I went through with the broken bolt in the front-end steering pedestal.

I also decide that this system of mine may not be the best one. I may stick with it, but it really isn't very bright. The process of working on a tractor for me looks like this:

Flow Chart for System A

A.

DISMANTLE → DISMANTLE → DISMANTLE → DISMANTLE → DISMANTLE → DISMANTLE → DISMANTLE →

GOLDEN TURN-AROUND!

→ RE-ASSEMBLE → REASSEMBLE → REASSEMBLE → REASSEMBLE → REASSEMBLE → REASSEMBLE.

The day I start working on a tractor, there is a world of things to be done—or rather undone, and I keep doing (or undoing) those things until they are all done and the tractor is completely dismantled, whereupon I reach THE MOMENT OF THE GOLDEN TURN-AROUND (or maybe not, as you have just seen). Then all at once everything is ready to be done again and I start doing things until they are all done and the tractor is finished.

There are a lot of disadvantages to this method—at The Moment of Golden Turn-Around, for example, the shop is hopelessly cluttered because the tractor is totally dismantled. Another problem is the frustration that comes inevitably from having just one or two things standing in the path of further progress. In fact, the only advantages I can think of in this old system of mine are that one does get to celebrate The Moment of the Golden-Turn Around (in this case, maybe twice) and there are certain organizational advantages to thinking of only one thing at a time, especially at my age.

During the day, as I scrape and scrub and sweep the floor I decide that for a lot of people (maybe even me) another system might work better, one that looks like this:

Flow Chart for System B

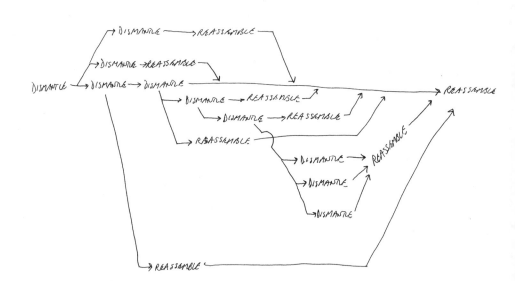

The notion here is I would take off one component at a time, work on that component, take off damaged or worn parts, put on new or repaired parts and *then* move on to the next component. The problem with that approach, however, is that to get, for example, to the clutch, I still would have to dismantle most of the tractor, at least breaking it down into components. I suppose I could then use winches, dollies, stands, and other devices to remove various components—front end, cooling system, engine, clutch, rear end, transmission—to a corner of the shop or another part of the farm until I come back through the process to them. Probably the biggest advantage to that system would be that I would be able to celebrate hundreds of little Moments of Golden Turn-Around rather than just one big one.

The place where this process would be most obviously, tactically superior is with the engine. Instead of taking apart the engine and having pistons, sleeves, valves, head, all that stuff scattered around the shop in cans and boxes, hanging on pegs and hooks, I would rebuild the engine as I finish things like the oil pump, carb, rocker arms, etc., and then tuck it away to be re-inserted onto the tractor when I finished the same sort of mini-procedures with the transmission, rear end, brakes, those sorts of things.

Sure, there'd be no one single, orgasmic Moment of the Golden Turn-Around but instead of obsessing with one broken and stuck bolt, I could be taking care of other things that need to be done. While tearing apart the Woodpecker's transmission and PTO, for example, I could have been re-assembling the engine. Instead of sitting here now with one bolt between me and everything else, I could be well along the way to finishing the tractor and having it ready to go even if that one blasted bolt under the differential were still stuck.

This means I would have to be thinking about dealing with all the problems of getting the engine back together while also mulling over my transmission problems. That would be enough of a muddle even if I could work in the shop almost every day. With my schedule of having long gaps between my shop days, how can I keep everything in mind that I need to remember, even if I keep a close and careful record of where I am and what I'm doing? Unless I pledged myself to finishing each component job before caving into the temptation of working on the next one while I'm waiting for parts or ideas or advice for the first. I don't know. Maybe it'll work for you. I'm going to give it a try on my next tractor project.

A couple more tries at the broken bolt (nothing) and I give up for the day, not quite as cheery as I started.

> Day 24 hours   3.0
> Total project hours   74.0,
> not counting the time I've spent think-
> ing, stewing, and worrying about it all,
> which amounts, I would guess, to three
> or four normal lifetimes.

DAY 25

Unfinished Business

WELSCH WEATHER REPORT

Finally, a cold, misty, dark day, my idea of a good day for shop work.

I STOKE THE STOVE, TURN ON THE LIGHTS, and stare at that blasted broken mounting bolt on the rear end. The best part of the afternoon is that Linda comes out to the shop to join me, doing sketches for *Old Tractors and the Men Who Love Them*. The shop is not exactly a place of great comfort for her. It's dirty and smelly, she says. I counter that I am too, and she changes the subject.

I do enjoy the solitude and privacy that is usual in the shop, but it's nice to have her here for an hour or so, sketching quietly while I bang at the bolt and cuss. Finally she has enough and leaves me to the really dirty and smelly job of cleaning the last problems with the transmission (the inside of the clutch housing is filthy) and steering pedestal, pulling off the front hubs to check bearings and seals and renewing the old, water-saturated grease, replacing a broken grease zirk . . .

Thank goodness, the front wheel bearings and seals seem to be in very good shape. Since the front wheel hubs are not the same, someone did some work on this machine's front end, and from what I see, I'd guess it wasn't too long before the tractor was abandoned in the wood lot where Jim Stromp found it.

When you think about it, that sort of thing is inevitable. On a working machine like a tractor, there are always repairs and maintenance to be done. So, you're out in the field one spring and a front wheel bearing gives out. You get the tractor back to the shop and put on a new bearing—not a big job but a necessary one. You go back out to the field and work a couple days—and the engine goes to pot . . . a broken rod, burned main bearing, shot clutch, something big like that. You decide you've had enough in the way of repairs on this old wreck. It's time for a new tractor. You aren't going to get much in the way of a trade-in, so you park the old Allis back behind the chicken house, figuring maybe some day you'll fix it up, or scavenge the starter off of it, or cut it up for scrap.

It never happens, and 30 years later, someone buys the old wreck at a farm sale (probably for more than you paid for it new), and hauls it home to rebuild it. That guy, when he opens things up, finds a shaggy engine . . . but new bearings in the front end.

I once bought a wrecked Allis WC at a farm auction and hauled it home. I was looking it over when I happened to notice the oil pan was held on by only four pan bolts and they weren't even very tight. Now, if you have spent much time working on tractors, you know what that means: someone worked on this machine, gave up, and tacked the oil pan back on just to get it off the ground, maybe to hide the big problems inside that engine. This is not a good sign, I thought.

I had no intention of starting to work on this particular tractor with the loose oil pan, but I couldn't resist the temptation to take a look. I took out the four bolts and dropped the pan. Sure as heck, there was no oil there, but there were the rest of the pan bolts. I turned my light up into the crankshaft, cylinder bottoms, oil pump, and piston rods. Well, look at that!—new bearings and new sleeves. I'll bet when I do get around to completely dismantling that engine, I find new piston rings and maybe even new pistons. Whoever was doing the overhaul on that engine did all the hard and expensive work, but never got the last little part of the job finished for some reason—maybe he couldn't find a gasket for the pan before he was called into the army or lost the farm or died or got a new tractor or ran off to Vegas with that cute new school-marm. Whatever the case, for the $90 I paid for the tractor, I picked up a minimum of $300 worth of new parts. With the Woodpecker, the treasure seems to be the new bearings and seals in the front hubs.

It's good I can find something cheering in the process because all afternoon I continue to bang on that broken bolt on the rear end with no progress. I think the next step is to try to weld a nut on what's left of the stub. I don't look forward to that, because welding upwards is something I have been warned about a lot by welding veterans. Worse, I have the uneasy feeling that what I'll wind up doing is twisting that blasted bolt off in the rear end casting and have to go through the whole extraction process again. I resolve that I will mitigate the frustration by starting on rebuilding the engine, foregoing a second Gold Moment of Turn-Around.

> Day 25 hours   3.0
>
> (Maybe I should count those three hours as six, since all the while I was cleaning and scraping, I was also fussing about that broken bolt.)
>
> Total project hours   77.0

Welding, PTOs, and Rock 'n' Roll

I AM SO EXCITED ABOUT THE EXTRA LONG time I have at my disposal, I start the stove up the night before so the shop will be warm right away, first thing in the morning. There are still no signs of movement in the stuck bolt in the rear end, and I decide I am going to ignore it for a while. The next warm day, I'll weld a nut to it and see if the heat and added leverage help. I don't like to weld when the shop is closed because the place fills with smoke almost immediately, so I'll do my best to ignore that problem for a while.

Instead I decide to devote the day to getting a PTO transmission ready to go since I can't fill the main transmission until I get that job done. The PTO case that came with The Woodpecker had cracked in a tidy, little square pattern on the bottom, and at this point I have pulled two cases off two parts tractors. My plan is two-fold: first, I'm going to clean one of the alternative cases, check it for seal leaks, bearings, that sort of thing, and if it is in good shape, install it. If it isn't in good shape, I may order replacement parts and move to something else while I wait, or I'll clean up the third PTO unit. Secondly, I am going to experiment with the bum PTO box, the one that came with The Woodpecker, by making my first effort to braze shut the freeze break. If it works, well, I'll have a spare PTO case on my parts shelves.

I spend the morning cleaning away at the alternate PTO unit, listening to rock 'n' roll (I know it's only rock 'n' roll, but I like it, like it, yes, I do!), and generally enjoying the coziness of the shop. The alternate PTO unit seems to be in pretty good shape—the bearings feel solid enough, the gears are not damaged, and the case is . . . Jeez, this case is cracked too, in exactly the same little square pattern on the bottom. Damn.

I finish the cleaning job (just because I can't use this casting as is doesn't mean it won't be useful somewhere else down the line, as parts or even as a unit, if I get to the point where I can weld or braze cast-iron well) and put the unit aside. I pull out the third PTO in the row and start on it, this time cleaning the bottom first. Damn, damn, and double damn. This one is broken too, in the same little square pattern.

"What a coincidence!" you're thinking. "What are the chances of someone running into three cast-iron power-take-off boxes, all cracked in exactly the same way?!"

Well, the chances are excellent. In fact, I'm willing to bet that if I went to Jim Stromp's salvage yard at this very moment and took off three more PTO units from Allis WCs, at least one of them would have that nasty little square crack. Chances are good that two of them do, and it would not be at all surprising if all three were. It's not so much a design fault as a natural consequence: drops of water seep into the transmission through cracks in the shift lever boot—that little rubber cup at the base of the gearshift lever. The water goes right to the bottom of the transmission—which is the PTO case. Over the years the water builds up until it reaches the bottom of the gears. The next time it freezes, it has no where to go but down, against that cast-iron bottom—where it breaks out a neat little square. As a natural consequence, Allis WC PTO transmission cases become rare (and expensive) items.

I guess I'll have to learn how to braze or weld cast-iron pretty darn soon. I have read the books and talked with the old timers so I have some idea how it goes. Let's face it, brazing is not exactly brain surgery. I use a grinder to cut a little V along the crack on the first case, the one that came off The Woodpecker and is now all nicely cleaned up. I warm up the case on the woodstove and fire up the welder. (I am using a carbon arc torch rather than a gas set-up.) At first things do not go very well—the brazing rod sticks, drops gobs, puddles up . . . and I'm frustrated. In a matter of minutes, things begin to go better, and before long, the repair looks pretty good. I grind down the built up braze and spot a few holes and cracks. I give the torch and brazing rod another try to close them up.

It looks good, but as the unit cools off, the brazing pulls away from the casting in a hairline crack. Well, this may or may not work. There is another possible direction, even if I can't get the crack brazed shut right off the bat. It is at least sealed up well enough, for example, that an internal sealer might work—gas tank sealer, or a thin layer of silicon, or JB Weld. Those may not be the best solutions, but they could be workable.

It is especially important here to remember again how this tractor will be used—strictly as a toy. It'll never spend another day plowing, it won't be used as a heavy puller. I'll drive it into town for fun, maybe use it to tow-start another tractor. It's entirely possible that for the rest of the Woodpecker's life, the PTO will never be used except maybe, if I ever get the job done, to run a corn picker by way of a demonstration at a champagne party.

Yet, I would rather do this job right. So, over the next couple weeks I'm going to work on at least one of the other PTO cases with a nickel welding rod. Dan Selden drops by the shop, looks the situation over, and suggests that as a possible course of action. I'll give it a shot. I want to do this job right, but I also want to get the job done, and sometimes getting it done is doing it right. The only thing I can do at this point is to clean up the other two PTOs so I can weld, braze, seal, patch—whatever—farther down the line. Maybe by then I'll know how to weld or braze better. Now that I know the problem, I'll thumb through some of my welding books for advice.

It probably sounds like a frustrating day to you, and in some ways it was, but I learned some things and I tried some things. I now know what the problems are and I have some ideas about what I can to do solve them. Wouldn't it be nice if that happened every day? Sometimes, we learn as much by a failure as we do by a success. If, for example, I jimmy with a carburetor and darned if it doesn't work perfectly, I know roughly how a working carb looks. What I don't know is the hundreds of ways it shouldn't look. I'll probably still have to learn those models down the road. Is that Zen tractor restoration, or what?

| Day 26 hours | 6.0 |
| Total project hours | 83.0 |

Spontaneous Combustion

If you're at all like me and Lovely Linda, you'd rather play things on the safe side and worry about things that don't need worrying about rather than ignore them. The following letter from John Mason of Key Largo, Florida, therefore, is very interesting, but hasn't changed my habits at all. I'm still not comfortable with that tub of greasy, oily rags piling up in the shop! Isn't it nice, though, that John took the time to write?

Dear Rog,

I have read your book *Old Tractors and the Men Who Love Them* and really enjoyed it. When it arrived days ago I couldn't put it down. It took me back to the farm I came from, which was mostly apple and a lot of other crops in Connecticut.

We had five farm tractors—three Fords, one Farmall M, and a Cub. I really wish I had them now.

In your book you mentioned storage of used, oily rags could possibly spontaneously combust. I am a State of Florida certified arson investigator and I would like to let you know that it definitely will not occur with the hydrocarbon (lubricating) oils and is not expected with most fats and oils found in a household. But I have heard that animal and vegetable oil soaked rags stored in metal cans will combust in about 30 days. So don't try this at home because these oils burn very hot.

Some oils in which spontaneous combustion is commonly noted are the drying oils used in paint. Drying oils like linseed, tung, fish, and soybean harden by oxidation in the fatty acid chains of the oil, and heat is generated. For combustion to occur, the presence of considerable oil, spread in a film so as to have access to sufficient oxygen or air and yet surrounded by enough insulation to allow heat to accumulate, is required. Such a situation can occur in a large pile of "oily" cotton rags, wet with drying oils, such as may accumulate during painting. It sounds like you don't paint. The National Fire Protection Association has rated many common oils and products (both natural and synthetic) with respect to their susceptibility to self-ignition and can be found in the Fire Protection Handbook, 16th edition, Quincy, Mass, 1988, Chapter 5, pages 130-136. My opinion is to store them in a metal container with a lid to keep sparks from entering while welding, grinding, etc., but not to worry about them burning by themselves. Or dispose of them properly.

—John Mason

Well, okay, but . . . I'm still nervous. I keep my "keeper" rags—mostly towels, washcloths, and napkins I use to wipe my hands after I have used hand cleaner—in a metal tub and I haul them to the house and launder them as often as Lovely Linda leaves town for a day or two, since she's not all that crazy about me using her washing machine for my "rags." I toss throw-away rags—the ones I use to clean parts, mop up oil stains from the floor, that sort of thing—directly into my iron shop stove.

My Idea of Fun

WELSCH WEATHER REPORT

It's Sunday, so my start in the shop is a little late, but the shop has stayed warm enough that I don't have to wait for the stove to get to work for me to get to work.

I THINK I'LL START TO PUT THE ENGINE back together—the engine that was on The Woodpecker when I got it. Kenny Porath has said he'll come over and help me weld the cracked block if I clean it up real well. He prefers to grind his own V along the crack, and that's fine with me: it'll give me a chance to see how an expert does it.

I start the day by cleaning the crankshaft, which is something I really enjoy. With kerosene and Scotchbrite padding I take years of dirt and grease off the crankshaft, bearing caps, and bearings. I think what I like about the process is that it's quiet—I just sit at my bench listening to the Sunday news programs and then an Indy car race—and I can see the progress. Bright, shiny metal appears from under the dirt, and just *seems* happy.

I use kerosene as a solvent (and have an exhaust fan opposite my work table so the fumes are pulled away from me and out of the shop), cleaning with dental tools, toothbrushes, and scouring pads (soft enough not to scratch the metal). I scrub the parts in a shallow nylon tray and a couple coffee cans. I use the kerosene again and again until all the 'sene is worn out of it. I let it settle over night in one of the coffee cans, then pour off the cleanest of it, using the filth in the bottom to start the day's fire. (I know the dangers of this—I lost a grandfather to a kerosene fire—but with care, it can be done safely.) I start cleaning parts with the icky kerosene, mostly to loosen the tough dirt and grease. When everything is scrubbed loose, I squirt light amounts of brand new kerosene onto the part from a squirt can, thereby adding a little new, cleaner oil to the inventory. Finally, I wipe the piece clean with a clean cloth. Sure is pretty.

Next I work on the block, scrubbing it inside and out with kerosene, brushes, and pads. I wipe it clean with soft, clean rags. I use a scouring pad on a mandrel with a variable speed electric drill to clean machined surfaces to bright. As I'm cleaning, I note that the block is cracked between each of the cylinder sleeve holes. There is only a narrow bridge of cast-iron between the sleeve holes and each one is cracked at the narrowest neck. The first time I saw a block like this, my heart sank. I had just read in a restoration guide somewhere that when you wind up with a block with an internal crack like that, you might just as well throw it on the scrap pile.

At the time, I looked the situation over, saw I really didn't have much of a choice since this was the only block I had. Anyway I couldn't figure out what difference it would make, since a sleeve makes a cylinder-piston combination a closed system anyway, the block serving only to hold it in place. I put the tractor back together—that was Old Faithful, the first tractor I worked on years ago—and of course it ran fine.

Now, remember that cracked PTO casing? Well, I have now opened maybe 20 Allis WC engines . . . and every blasted one of them was cracked between the sleeve holes. Every one. In fact, if I ever open up one of these things and find a block that *isn't* cracked like that, I'll probably wonder what's wrong. [Author's Note: In the two years since I first wrote these words, I have indeed found two blocks with uncracked sleeve bridges. I cannot for the life of me figure out how that could have happened.] The Woodpecker block is also cracked inside on the castings between the sleeve holes *at the bottom of the sleeve*. This could be something more of a problem since this piece of metal separates the coolant around the cylinder sleeves from the oil underneath. I've never really paid much attention to this part of the casting—the bottom sleeve casting—so maybe they've all been cracked too. I don't know. I am concerned that cracks here might let water from above leak into the oil pan below, especially around the O-rings. There are some terrific cooling system sealants these days, so I hope I can get around that problem if it shows up down the line. I may try a little silicon sealer on both sides of the cracks before I close up the engine. [As it turned out, I didn't do this risky move.]

I scrub the sealing surfaces where the block meets the sleeve at the top and the bottom with kerosene and Scotchbrite™ pads, a wire brush, and finally a polishing pad on a drill until they are shiny and clean, ready for the sleeves. Even though this part of the block is bathed with oil from

THE WHOLE TOWN'S ROOTING FOR YOU ON THIS LATEST TRACTOR PROJECT, ROGER...

...JUST DON'T BE IN SUCH A RUSH TO FINISH. IT GIVES US ALL SO MUCH TO TALK ABOUT.

MEETING THE LOCAL FANS...

below and coolant from above, it is nonetheless immediately adjacent to the cylinder wall and has to be a mighty hot location.

I clean up the parts of the oil pressure adjustment and re-insert them in the engine block. Boy, that feels good, seeing parts going back into the block. It won't be long before I put the sleeves and the crankshaft in place. Then it will start to look like an engine again. There is a problem of priorities here, however. I don't want to make the welding job on the block complicated (or impossible) by putting parts like the crankshaft in the way. I think I'll just start lining up the cleaned parts to be inserted once Kenny P. comes over and welds that block for me.

The rest of the afternoon I clean the timing gear cover, which is a real mess, inside and out. The governor mechanism is sticky, so I give special attention to it. The hole in the cover where the throttle rod exits is badly worn and the throttle rod therefore wobbles and jams. I'm going to think about shimming it up, maybe with a make-shift insert. It's completely out of sight, back behind the radiator, so it won't be noticeable (but everyone will know if the throttle doesn't work right).

The day is over, and again, although I haven't gotten all that much done, I whistle my way back to the house. I am making small steps, and best of all, they are steps toward putting the machine back together. When Dan Selden dropped by today, we looked at the pathetic frame of a tractor sitting on its jack stands and I wondered aloud, "Do you think this thing will ever run again, yet by September?"

"Well, about all I can say is, you sure did take her apart, all right."

Yeah, Dan, and over the next half year, I'm going to put her back together, you watch and see. I have a couple bad months coming up because I know I am going to be working full tilt and probably won't have a day in a month to work on the Woodpecker, but my heart will be out here in the shop with this dirty, rusty iron. She will run again.

> Day 27 hours   6.0
> Total project hours   89.0
>   (Frankly, I don't think that's all that
>   much—a total, after all, only 11 full
>   days, not even two weeks. All that
>   pleasure, and so little invested.
>   Yessir, this is my idea of fun.)

Rocker Hygiene

WELSCH WEATHER REPORT

After a howling Nebraska snowstorm, a bitter cold settles over the farm.

I WENT OUT TO THE MACHINE SHED early in the morning, thinking I'd start up the International tractor and plow the snow that blew in knee-deep overnight, but it was so cold—well below zero—I couldn't get it to start. I guess the school bus will just have to plow its own way in.

A *great* day, therefore, to spend in the shop.

Unfortunately, however, I have a day's worth of work in the office, so I don't get into the shop until late afternoon. After a long break from the task, I try again to break loose that blasted broken bolt under the differential case but it is no more cooperative than before. Damn. I'll have to wait until the day is warm enough to open the big doors and weld a nut on it. If that doesn't work, I'll have to drill it out.

I spend about an hour cleaning on the rocker arms, a task I find very pleasant. The dirt on the rockers is usually well soaked in oil and rubs off fairly easily, so things move along quickly. Moreover, it's *ugly* dirt, so the shiny metal is all the prettier when the dirt comes off. I carefully dismantle the entire assembly and line up the parts on my work bench so I can put them back together in the same order. As so often happens, I'm surprised to find that whoever did this job last put the exhaust and intake valve rockers back on the rocker assembly bar in no particular order. I don't suppose it makes much difference, therefore, and I'll put them back on the way they were rather than the way they're supposed to be. The guy who did this, after all, might have had a reason I can't spot right off the bat. Or maybe he didn't know there's a difference. Oh well . . .

It's only an hour later when I go to the house, not nearly enough done. After supper, and the television news, I make one of my rare evening jaunts out to the shop. If the shop is cozy on a cold, snowy day, it's all the more so on a cold, snowy night. I put another hour into the rocker assembly and finish it up. I'll probably sleep well with visions of that pretty, shiny rocker arm assembly on my shop bench dancing through my dreams. Boy, I hope I eventually see these arms dancing up and down on top of a running engine!

Day 28 hours	2.0
Total project hours	91.0

Norwegian Torque Wrench Techniques

I got a couple of useful letters from Ross Rash of Bloomington, Minnesota. He wrote me about my frustration in breaking loose difficult nuts and bolts and his frustrations in shaking loose a difficult wife. And an unsettling bit of information about my misconception that kerosene is a lot less dangerous than gasoline around the shop. Begin at the beginning with Ross Rash letter number one:

Dear Roger,

As a 66-year-old relic from Gordon, Nebraska, that has retired as an engineer and is in need of some R&R (Repair and Rehabilitation) himself, I would like to let you know how much I enjoyed your recent book on old tractors and their care and feeding. I have memories of wearing a fine polish on the seats of many pair of Levis from the iron seat of an old Farmall F-20, which I believe is still in use with a Stack Hand bolted onto it.

Over the years I have worked upon many old and not so old Mercedes automobiles and engines. One of my more useful discoveries was the "Norwegian Torque Wrench," which is unexcelled in removing round cornered nuts, bolts, and hex head cap screws with stretched holes, as well as inaccessible nuts, bolts, and cap screws. It is also effective in removing any of the above items that will not respond to breaker bars with three-foot extensions. The "Norwegian Torque Wrench" is sold for $25 to $35 under the trade name of "Air Chisel." Its effectiveness is due to the high impact forces it generates that can loosen "stuck" items without twisting them off, and to the fact that the chisel blade makes its own notch in the item to be rotated from a wide range of angles that might be otherwise impossible with conventional wrenches. For example, my wife's 1987 Mercedes 190E had a deceased hydraulic shock absorber on the idler pulley for the serpentine fan belt, which is over six feet in length (the belt, that is). These gadgets are normally installed while the engine is on an assembly line by a worker with a pneumatic wrench with a hex head bit and uses eight-millimeter drive cap screws of mild steel. Once they are installed in the car, you are limited to an Allen wrench with a five-inch "handle" that reams out the socket without loosening the screw. After exhausting my fingers, and vocabulary, I reached for the Air Chisel and gave the offending cap screw a couple of one second zaps which rotated it a half turn, from which point it could be removed with fingers.

Another little appreciated fact is that kerosene explosions have probably launched as many people into the next world as have gasoline fires/explosions. The ignitable air/fuel ratio range of kerosene is about twice that of gasoline. It is not as volatile and has a higher ignition temperature than gasoline but the ignitable range and the opinion that kerosene is safe will result in explosions where gasoline would only smell bad.

Best regards—Ross Rash

I wrote to Ross asking for some clarification about his Norwegian Torque Wrench Technique and what he *does* use for cleaning parts, and he responded . . .

Roger,

Regarding the Norwegian Torque Wrench, the secret is to aim an [air] chisel at an angle that will unscrew the offending fastener while it is pounding on it. I made this momentous discovery while intending to use the chisel as a "nut-splitter" in a location that could not be reached with a splitter which I couldn't find anyway.

I have been using number one or number two diesel fuel for cleaning old engines and other parts from the lower regions of automobiles for years. It has a better penetrating characteristic than gasoline or kerosene because it has lower volatility and soaks in rather than evaporating. A couple of soaks with diesel juice and a good hosing down will usually removed 10 to 30 years worth of cooked on oil, dirt, and grease. The downside is that the stuff stinks. Number two diesel juice is essentially the same as number two burner fuel except that burner fuel may have no additives for engine use. It is also hard stuff to ignite.

—Ross Rash

Broken Differential Mounting: Bolt 1, Rog 0

WELSCH WEATHER REPORT

Another beautiful warm day.

I THROW OPEN THE DOORS TO THE SHOP and line up all my welding chores and exercises—one of which is to try to weld a nut and washer on the reluctant, broken bolt in Woodpecker's differential casting. I do all my other jobs first—repair a broken barbecue grill, cut the top off a small metal barrel, make a rod holder for my welding table—and then turn to The Woodpecker. For two hours—the whole second half of the morning—I try to weld the nut and washer on the broken bolt with absolutely no luck. For one thing, I'm welding uphill, which is never easy, but the thing just doesn't seem to want to cooperate. After lunch, I give it one more try, again without success. Without even considering where I go from here, I decide to make the day into something useful and forget about that damned broken bolt for the time being.

And that's what I do. First, since I have the welder working already, I take the second cracked PTO case and decide to try my hand at welding cast-iron—again, a tough task even for experienced welders. I heat the case on the wood stove and warm it a little further with a small propane torch to reduce the stress induced in the cast-iron by heating one small part of it to such a high degree. I weld small, quarter-inch lengths at a time, trying to avoid letting the weld site get too hot, just like the book tells me. Things go well. The weld holds, the case it tight, and it looks good. Whew, the day may not be a total loss after all.

Then I set up my work bench so I can watch a NASCAR race on my little shop television, turn on the exhaust fan, and set up my brushes, cups, picks, and scrapers so I can clean piston sleeves.

Shop electronics are a very delicate part of the diplomacy of tractor restoration, if you haven't figured that out already. Thing is, you want to have a comfortable shop with all kinds of things to make your time out there a pleasure, but you don't want to get things so comfortable that your spouse comes to suspect you're getting TOO comfortable. I have a small, battered television set, for example, that makes it clear that this is not a watching TV but a background TV. The reception is too snowy and staticky to make prolonged viewing possible; it lets me keep up with a car race or a particularly moving soap opera installment, but it's not the sort of thing I'm likely to be captivated by while trying to weld a broken frame.

To my mind a little refrigerator would be nice but 1) it would make the place look far more like a boys' club than a work station in Linda's eyes, and 2) it would remove any excuses I currently have for not offering drop-in buddies a cold beer. With my friends, I figure a shop refrigerator would cost me in the neighborhood of $10,000 a year. I can do without that.

What I can't do without is my sound system. I love rock 'n' roll—loud—and my shop is where I can indulge that weakness. Linda maintains that I come out of my shop after an afternoon with ZZ Top played at ear-shattering volume looking like a victim of shell shock—glazed-over eyes, shaking hands, weak bladder, stone deaf—but I love it. So, I have a good, big sound system. I prefer my CD player to the tape deck because by the time I handle an audio tape three or four times while I'm cleaning parts with kerosene, for some reason they don't play quite the same again. The CDs are locked in a closed selector and all I have to do is poke a button, or better yet, start the series and play through the entire dozen or so CDs I own, without touching any delicate surfaces with my indelicate fingers.

Appliances such as an exhaust fan are matters of survival, salvation from asphyxiation and solvent explosions. The guys in town think I'm a sissy for having an air conditioner, but I have one and I turn it on and I'm grateful every time I work in comfort on a fiercesomely hot summer day. I cannot for the life of me understand why anyone would want a telephone in a shop unless the bell has been removed. In summary, that's my work environment. Now, back to work.

I am still very much in the experimenting stages of figuring out how to clean things like sleeves. I have tried some fairly dangerous substances like oven cleaner, lime remover, gasket remover, and muriatic acid. (If you try stuff like this, be sure you have good ventilation and are wearing protective gloves and eye guards. I have tried a wide variety of protective gloves and have wound up quite content with regular, grocery-store variety dish-washing gloves.) I find that kerosene is still about as good as anything for getting the soft, oily stuff off, and then it is a matter of wire brushes, Scotchbrite, wire wheels, and composition abrading wheels.

I use the abrading wheels on a variable speed electric drill, being careful to keep the speed down; if a wire brush gets away from you and whisks across the back of your hand, it leaves some kind of mat burn! Abrasive pads *eat* meat. I use dental picks to pick loose stuck bits of O-ring rubber. If there is some really hard carbon or burnt oil in the O-ring grooves, I use a round, rat-tail file to work it loose—being careful that I am only removing the carbon and rubber and not putting a divot in the sleeve. For really bad cases, I put the file in a drill chuck and *very gently* work the drill around the grooves. This is a risky way to clean the grooves since you can easily damage the sleeves, but if you're careful, it can work miracles.

By the time the day is over I feel I have accomplished something, despite the frustrations of my nemesis, The Broken Differential Mounting Bolt. I did some cast welding, cleaned two sleeves, tidied things up in the shop, and helped the LaBonte boys through a tough race.

Day 29 hours	5.5
Total project hours	96.5

The Fickle Gods of Tractor Restoration

WELSCH WEATHER REPORT

Another gorgeous day, and once again I am in the luxurious situation of having two days in a row in the shop.

MY PALS DAN AND DENNIS DROP by for morning coffee and in the course of conversation I explain the trouble I've been having with The Broken Differential Bolt. "Let's go take a look at it," one of them says, and we head out to the shop. It turns out that my problem is indeed the part about welding *up*, and Dennis says I probably should have been using DC-setting on the welder . . . that might have helped. They look over the stub of the bolt and Dan asks, "Tried a pipe wrench yet?" Dan's a plumber; he *would* think of a pipe wrench.

"That's a pretty small stub for a pipe wrench, isn't it?" I ask, dubious.

"Well, it's worth a shot."

I hand him a pipe wrench. He tightens it down on the bolt, and the sound of it snapping loose echoes through the shop. Dan twists the bolt out, and we find that it had been cross-threaded in its hole, maybe for the past 40 years. No wonder it was so reluctant.

The real question about this moment of triumph, however, is, why, after all my work, did it finally break loose when Dan tugged at it? Did all my previous banging, squirting, twisting, heating, and cooling lead up to this, or was it all futile tinkering? Was Dan's pull on the bolt a little different than mine, just different enough to break the thing loose? Why wasn't it me who felt it break loose after all these weeks? Wouldn't my feeling of victory have been far more than Dan's? Doesn't matter. He took it out. I didn't. That's the way the tractor gods work, that's why, and I better get used to it. Maybe you should too.

I'm not the one to explain this sort of thing. My feeling about religion is that the more anyone claims they know about the will of God, the more profound their ignorance is likely to be. Here in my little town of Dannebrog, the people who go to church regularly are the very folks who seem most in the need of spiritual help, and the ones who never go are the folks who seem to understand the most about what is spiritually right and wrong, good and bad.

I suspect it may be the same with the gods of Rust and Iron. I don't know what pleases those powers, which probably puts me closer to the ultimate truth than those who think they know it all. Why did that broken bolt turn out for Dan but not for me? Well, just because. I try to remain pure of heart, but sometimes, most of the time, maybe all the time, that's just not enough. It wasn't in the case of that bolt.

The triumph certainly sets things up for a grand day. I spend the rest of it cleaning sleeves. Dan drops back in for a chat later, and Kenny Porath comes through to do some work on my working tractor, the International, and then he looks over the cracked block I am planning to put into The Woodpecker. We talk about how we are going to approach that chore in the next few weeks. I go to the house for supper pooped but cheerful.

Day 30 hours	4.0
Total project hours	100.5

Studs 0, Rog 2

WELSCH WEATHER REPORT

A lovely spring day, hints of rain, nicely cool.

I FINISH OFF THE CLEANING OF THE LAST two sleeves. Now they are all shiny and oiled standing in a row, ready to be re-inserted into the block as soon as Kenny P. comes over and welds the block. Actually, I could probably weld the block myself but I want the chance to see how a real mechanic attacks the problem. After I finished in the shop a week ago, Day 30, I put water in each of the PTO transmission cases I tried to repair—one brazed, the other nickel welded. To my goofy delight, not a drop leaked from either one. Yeah, I'm a welder!

I don't have much time today so I'm not going to take on any big jobs. When I write, which I've been doing for 30 years, I never stop in a "good place"—the end of a chapter, the end of an idea, just before I have to start a difficult passage. I have found that when I do that, it is almost impossible to get started again. So now I turn off the word processor and leave the office only when things are going really well and I desperately want to keep going. That's the sort of spirit that keeps me wanting to get back in here writing.

That's not the way it goes in the shop, I find, because it is more often than not the difficult jobs that I find the most interesting. I like to walk away from the shop with a task finished, knowing that the next time I come out, I'll be starting a whole new adventure. So, knowing I have only a couple hours to work with today, I clean up the rubble from previous days, put away tools, sweep out both bays, and take a look at two rear wheel studs with nuts stuck on them.

I took these babies off when I first rolled the tractor into the shop, many months ago. I worked and worked at them then, without success. I left them in a margarine tub of kerosene for the past six months, and now I'm going to give them another shot. I was almost at the point of giving up and throwing them into the iron bin, but boy, I hate to lose any parts.

I fasten the nut tightly in my bench vise and tighten down a pipe wrench on the shank of the lug. I pull as hard as I can. My arm pops, my back cracks . . . and the lug moves in the nut! Oh man, what a sweet feeling! I reset the wrench and pull again. A terrible *squack* screams from the interior of that bolt and nut. I know that sounds crazy—"squack"—but it's true. That's the sound it makes.

The lug has turned a quarter turn in the nut. I spray the nut and lug with penetrating oil and turn it *back* into the hole. Again, I put everything into the wrench and there's that screaming noise again. Again, and again. The lug turns more and more easily, and then, after months and months of sitting in kerosene, decades of rusting on that lug, the nut is free, and I have rescued both the wheel lug and its nut.

I pull the second lug and stuck nut from the margarine tub, lock the nut in the vise, tighten the pipe wrench on the lug shaft, and throw my entire (and substantial) body into the wrench handle. The lug turns easily in the nut. By now I'm drenched in sweat, grinning with triumph. All the lugs are now off and separated from their nuts. Next trip out, I'll run chases over the lugs and through the nuts. It won't be long before I'll be putting the work wheels back on ol' Woodpecker, but for now I'll leave it up on jack stands so I have more room to move around the tractor. (My shop is larger than some but is still pretty cramped when there's a tractor sitting in one bay and a couple of engines in the other!)

Before I go in for supper, I pull out the filthy oil pan from the parts pile where it's been resting since I took it off the engine months ago. It's not just dirty and oily—the bottom is caked with a pasty, gooey mess of nut shells squirrels deposited in the engine, wasp nests, mouse droppings . . . really ugly. By now the day is warm enough that I can take the pan out onto the drive and scrape the nastiest parts out. I scrape the worst of the dirt off the outside of the pan, too. I rinse the pan with some junk gasoline I keep for just this purpose and set it out to dry until next trip out to the shop.

It's one of those days I simply hate to close the doors, but . . . it's time to go.

One of the reasons I swept up the shop the last time I was out here was because I knew a guest was coming who would want to see what I've been up to. Jim Harrison is one of my favorite non-tractor characters. He's a poet and screen-writer (*Wolf* and *Legends of the Fall* are a couple of his more popular works) and we know each other principally as writers. Jim also

knows how I feel about tractors. I took him out to see the shop and the state of The Woodpecker, and as he entered the door, he wafted the atmosphere of the room toward his nose with his hand as if he were appreciating a good wine. He smiled and nodded to me.

"Perfect," he said.

Who knows what caressed Jim's connoisseur-nose? The rich redolence of decaying rubber, rotten motor oil, and field-filth from old tractors? The sharp clean nose of new gaskets, Kroil oil, and welding flux? Years of frustration, sweat, burning flesh, and beer farts? All of those things? Something entirely different? In my modest opinion, all shops smell something alike—probably because of the above universals, and yet all are somehow distinct. Linda shares my feeling of the universal, "Rog," she says, "they all stink."

I don't need anyone's approval to enjoy what I do, but it's nice when someone you admire thinks you're doing all right! Harrison's appreciation of my shop's "distinktion" makes me proud. Maybe I should bottle the aroma of the shop in a fine, expensive cologne—"eau de querocine," maybe, or "Chanel Iron Number Four," or "Woof de Magneto."

Linda says no.

| Day 31 hours | 2.5 |
| Total project hours | 103.0 |

Head Surgery

I HAVE ALL DAY TODAY TO DEVOTE to the shop, so I'll take on something substantial—the head. As I move further and further from The Moment of the Golden Turn-Around, I am looking at parts and components I haven't seen for a long time. I took the head off this engine almost a half year ago, after all, and tucked it on wooden blocks under the bench where it's collected dust ever since.

Now, here it is again. Hmmm. I'd forgotten about the stuck studs, jumbled rocker arms, burnt valves, and wrong-sized spring. Double Hmmm.

Whenever I see something like that, a row of eight valve springs, seven of the same, right size and an eighth about half the diameter of the others, I try to imagine how that came to be. The farmer who owned this machine was probably in the middle of plowing or picking corn or cutting wood . . . or whatever, and the engine went sour on him. He could tell something was wrong with a valve, so he pulled the valve cover, and there it was—a broken valve spring. He made a quick trip to town, only to find that neither the local service station, or mechanic, or implement dealer had the right size valve spring. It would take two weeks for one to be delivered from Milwaukee, but the corn needed to be planted right away.

So he went to the local mechanic's shop and looked through his inventory. He sorted through a shelf of valve springs, maybe pawing over a box of old valve springs from under the work bench—Hupmobile parts, Minneapolis-Moline, Reo, DeSoto, Cockshutt. Nothing for an Allis WC, however. So he grabbed a spring that seemed the close to the right size, even though it was noticeably smaller, tossed it onto the eighth valve stem, shut up the cover, cranked her over, and went on with his tasks, thinking that maybe, the next time he needed to work inside that engine, he'd go ahead and order the right spring and get things straightened out again.

Thirty years later I open that very same valve cover and . . . there the problem is again, still uncorrected. What's truly remarkable to me about this is that this engine can run at all with wrong replacement parts slapped onto it. No doubt about it, these machines will put up with just about anything and still do what they have to do.

I pull the spark plugs from the head. They are pretty clean, considering that they haven't fired for almost a generation. Except the number one plug, and it is covered with rust and corrosion. That's how you can usually tell which cylinder is stuck in a stuck tractor motor—pull the plugs and one of them will be a lot dirtier than the others. That's your villain.

No matter where you stop an engine, one valve or another is certain to be open. Over years and years of time, minute quantities of moisture— sometimes substantial quantities—find their way into the cylinder and cause rust and corrosion (especially, it seems, where an aluminum piston is sitting for decades against a cast-iron sleeve or cylinder wall), and the engine is stuck, even if it wasn't before.

I can't help but wonder if it is only coincidence that in the case of The Woodpecker, the open valve that caused the problems was the self-same eighth valve with the oversized spring. Hard to tell at this point and it really doesn't matter. But this is almost assuredly the reason that one piston was hopelessly stuck in its sleeve.

Before I can pull the valves, I need to remove the stuck manifold lugs so they aren't in the way when I bring a valve spring compressor into play. I might as well prepare myself right now: I'm not going to get all of these rusted, bent old lugs out of this head intact. As much as I dread it, I know for sure I'm going to feel that sickening soft giving-way that comes when a lug is twisted off, usually inside the head. That feeling will mean I'm going to have to drill the blasted thing and carefully pick out the shreds, praying all the while that I don't botch up the threads.

I get out my three-cam stud puller and a ⅞-inch combination wrench. I spray all the lugs with penetrating solution and rap them firmly with a brass hammer. I let them sit for an hour or two while I take care of other jobs around the shop, return, spray them again, rap them harder, and apply the puller.

Remarkably, the first two lugs break loose and turn out smoothly. Just enough success to make me feel that maybe, just maybe, I'll get through this without twisting one off. And then, of course, I twist off the next two, with almost no pressure on the wrench at all. I console myself with the thought that they were so rusty and soft they would have twisted off no matter what I might have done. When I'm finished, three lugs are broken off, three come out whole. Well, there'll soon be some drilling and praying in the days to come, it seems.

Surprisingly, all the valves come out of the head fairly easily. The worst part of the operation is that when I put the valve spring compressor on the first valve, one of the keepers flies off somewhere and I can't find it for the life of me. Damn. Then one of the little wire C-clips that fit in a groove in the valve stem to keep it from slipping down into the cylinder if the keepers or spring fail flies off as I tug at it, hitting the lamp over my head, and then disappearing. Damn again. I get down on my hands and knees, knowing I'll never find the two lost pieces, but thank goodness I did that sweeping job in anticipation of Jim Harrison's visit, because I *do* find them! A good omen for the rest of the day, I tell myself.

From that point on, I am a lot more careful about easing the C-clips and keepers off the valve stems, you can be sure. For one thing, before I put the valve spring compressor on, I tap the spring and stem vigorously with a brass hammer. That way, the spring compressor doesn't break the spring loose, causing a jerk of the valve compressor tool and the spring, possibly throwing the keepers out. I have a wooden box that holds eight numbered old coffee cups exactly. As I take apart each valve, I put the parts into the appropriate cup to be cleaned later.

The rest of the morning and early afternoon I spend scraping, scrubbing, cleaning, brushing away the oil and dirt until the head is clean and shiny. The exhaust valve seats are pretty rough, but I think I will be able to smooth them out with valve-grinding compound. At least that's what I'll try. The exhaust valve guides are also badly burned and corroded and will have to be replaced. Not much of a job (knock on wood) but something that will have to be done. From this point on, my parts suppliers will be getting a lot of telephone calls.

Again, I don't want to take on a big job—like cleaning all the valve parts or grinding the valve seats—with the couple hours I have left, so instead I cut a new gasket for the PTO transmission box, which I should be able to mount under the transmission very soon now.

I really don't need a power take-off on all my tractors. Several in my collection have only a gaping hole under the transmission, the PTO having been robbed from the machine long before I came along. I imagine that a lot of the others are cracked, just like The Woodpecker's. I now have some confidence I can repair them, but I can imagine that I might also want to close the bottom of some transmissions with a plain plate rather than a PTO unit. The problem is, I don't have any such plates.

It's not that they're complicated—a simple, flat, rectangular plate with rounded corners and six ⅜-inch holes for mounting bolts. I spent a pleasant hour, therefore, cutting out a plate, grinding it down to size, and drilling mounting holes. Now I have a template and a big step up the next time I think I could use a plate. I'm not sure, but this may be the very first time I've actually made a "part" for one of my Allises.

Wonderful day in the shop.

Day 32 hours	6.0
Total project hours	109.0

Fancy Tractors

I mentioned in *Old Tractors* that as often as not, we do not choose what tractors we wind up loving, they choose us. I rambled on that if I had had some sort of choice, I probably would have chosen something with a name like Lamborghini or Porsche, both of whom make tractors. Well, I got a letter from a serviceman far out to sea to the effect that he had read my book, that he has a Lamborghini, and that his dream is to come back to the states and work on that machine.

In a later note he wrote some things that might be of value to many of you, whether the exotic nature of your tractor is that it is foreign, high-priced, very old, extremely rare, or not a standard feature of your particular local landscape.

Dear Roger,

I finally found the new pistons I needed for the Lamborghini Tractor, after going through some typical parts contortions. They were supposed to be available from Italy by the manufacturer, and a set was ordered and came in to the distributor that turned out to be nothing like the correct pistons. Then a second set was sent for, and they are still lost in the system somewhere between the U.S. and Italy. The estimated cost for the pistons was between $300 and $400 per piston, and that didn't include the rings or the pins. Looking at the potential bill of up to $2,000 didn't fill me with joy, so I searched for an alternative. I contacted a piston company in Los Angeles, and talked to them about the replacement pistons. After our conversation, I mailed one of the pistons out and the machinist looked it over and decided that he could make them without too much trouble. He quoted me a price of right around $600 for the pistons, pins, and rings, so I ordered them and they are coming home within the next few weeks. The cylinders will go to the local small engine shop and be bored oversize, and that will be what is needed to make the Lamborghini whole again. Of course, since the heads are off anyhow, they are getting the valves reground, but that's just normal since they are off the tractor. There are certain problems and hoops you must jump through when you own something a bit unusual, but so far none of them has been a total show stopper, and after I get the farm going to the point where it can support a tractor doing minimal returns, then the Lamborghini might get restored to a fare-thee-well and just be around to simply enjoy as a working toy. For the first few years, it's four-wheel drive system is going to be a blessing, and it will have an active working life until I manage to acquire something a bit bigger as the farm grows.

Well, I'll keep this short and get it on its way this afternoon, even though it probably won't leave the ship for a couple of days until we get a bit closer to Japan. Take care of yourself, and stay healthy. The key to health is more time in the shop and less on the road.

—Bob Burkhart

The Joy of Tinkering

WELSCH WEATHER REPORT

Cold and snowy. After having summer weather in February, we are now enjoying winter weather in March. Go figure. I thought I was just about done with the wood-stove for the year but I had to fire it up this morning and thaw out the water can on its top.

I SPEND ALL DAY GRINDING VALVES. I have a couple store-bought devices for grinding valves—these tools look like a short drill, but when you turn the handle, the bottom part makes a partial turn one way and then a partial turn the other. You're supposed to stick the bottom onto a valve (it has rubber sucker cups rather than drill bits), dab valve polishing goo on the edge of the valve seat, and turn away. I've never managed to get one of these things to work right. I wind up doing more spinning and jerking than the damned machine. Therefore, I prefer a straight piece of dowel with the sucker cup on the end, which I twirl between my hands. Works just fine, costs next to nothing.

Again, a real mechanic probably is wondering what I'm doing spending so many days on the simple job of tearing down and rebuilding an engine, something they do in a matter of hours. Well, for one thing, I'm being a little more careful than I am when I dismantle a parts machine. I'm packaging parts and hanging them up. I'm looking for damage and considering repairs. Moreover, it's one thing to take on a big project and go at it in a straight run, not having to clean up every hour or so, or get tools ready to go. The way I have to go after these things, I just barely get started before I have to stop, clean my tools, and put them away. A couple days, or weeks later, I come back out to the shop and start all over, and every new start requires time.

The main thing is, I'm having fun, not doing a job. When I come out to the shop, I tidy things up, put away tools, sip at my cup of coffee. I

look over what tasks lay ahead, turn on the radio, whistle, and bask in the glory of my shop and this old tractor. I take my time cleaning a valve port *because that's what this whole thing is about for me*. I'm not as much interested in *finishing* the job as I am in *doing* the job. So, I don't mind taking a pin-tipped dental tool and chip away at small flakes of hardened carbon or scrape away little dabs of dirt and grease for hours at a time. I savor the feeling of good tools in my hands. I admire shiny parts. I like to think about this tractor I've spent so much time getting to know. I enjoy every moment.

I imagine that a real mechanic who works in a shop to make a living, *to get things finished*, would go crazy watching me tinker around, but then I probably wouldn't enjoy it much if it were a job either. Tonight I come out of the shop more refreshed than when I started working.

Day 33 hours	6.0
Total project hours	115.0

The Sock-Dryer Syndrome

TODAY I WASH OFF THE HEAD AND valves to be sure I got all the highly abrasive valve-grinding compound off and reassemble the head. Everything is so pretty—shiny valves, clean springs, spotless head, immaculate rockers. You could handle these things with white gloves. Well, almost. An engine is still an engine. But the reassembled head is a pretty thing to look at, especially when I think about what this mess looked like when I started.

I replace the oversize valve spring and a couple missing retainer clips from valve stems. I didn't see what had happened to the clips when I took the head apart. On a different engine, I remember solving another such mystery. As I took that head apart, I wondered where a couple of the thin, little retainer clips might have gone, and then, when I turned it over and cleaned the tops of the cylinders, I could see where they had gone: The head had hundreds of little, semicircular divots in it. The clips had obviously fallen into the engine somehow, probably through the intake valve, and banged up and down a couple hundred times in the cylinder, maybe a couple thousand times, before being expelled. Man, a little piece of garbage inside an engine can really make a mess! Imagine what would happen if a valve dropped through! With that thought in mind, I make darned sure the valve keepers are firmly in place and that each valve stem has its retainer clip.

I haven't been able to find a source for the small wire clips that were original with the engines, so I have had to resort to C-clips. That can cause an occasional problem. The old wire clips are so low-profile, when I clamp down the spring with a valve-spring compressor, the top spring retainer slides easily over the clip so I can slide in the keepers—little metal keys like keystones in a stone arch that hold the valve firmly on the spring. But newer C-clips stick up above the valve stem far enough that the top spring retainer will not slide over. So, I have to slide the C-clip well down the stem of the valve, slip on the spring and top retainer, apply the valve spring compressor, slide in the keepers, and relax the valve-spring compressor. Now the valve is all set in the head—except for that C-clip, which is much too far down the valve stem. With a small screw driver I fish around through the spring coils and push the C-clip up the valve stem to its seat. It's a little more of a problem, but I sure wouldn't want to leave a valve without that clip on it.

Speaking of small parts, when I finish the springs, screw in the rocker bar lugs, and put the clean rocker bar on the head, I can't find the blast-ed four nuts that hold it on. They're not exotic parts—just plain old fine-thread nuts. I won't have any trouble finding replacements. But it still dri-ves me crazy I didn't put them away carefully enough so I can find them now that I need them. It's like the mystery of missing socks or ball-point pens, I suppose. Some things just disappear. I once lost a pecan pie and never found it again. Inside the house. Where could it possibly have gone? Beats me to this day.

Maybe some day I'll run across a little plastic bag with four valve cover nuts in it, but I doubt it. I'll bet I put those nuts down somewhere while I pulled the rocker bar off, thinking I would take care of them later. I never did and they wound up getting tossed into the nut bucket as stray parts. Remember: I never throw anything away. You could hold in one 60-gallon drum every broken or worn out part I've thrown away during six years of this work, and that includes a half dozen totaled manifolds and a hundred pounds of rusty baling wire. So, those nuts are in this shop somewhere.

I have a good morning but not enough time, considering how much I'm enjoying this task of putting ol' Woodpecker back together.

| Day 34 hours | 4.0 |
| Total project hours | 119.0 |

Mr. Clean

I HAVE A VERY SHORT COUPLE HOURS for the shop today. I spend them cleaning the oil pan and valve cover. It's not very inspirational, since it's more like washing dishes than mechanicking, but the job has to be done and for me there is still a lot of pleasure in taking a filthy piece of iron and making it shiny and clean. The morning is gone before I know it.

I'm caught in something of a log jam. I can't do much more on the engine until Ken comes over to weld the cracked block, and my weekends have been clogged up badly enough that we're not having much luck getting together to do it. Until then, I'm going to keep on cleaning parts (there's plenty of that to be done) and working on small projects— the water and oil pumps, the carb and magneto, radiator, sheet metal, steering . . . quite enough to keep me busy.

Moreover, I have a couple busy months coming up. (There's always this nuisance of having to earn a living!) So, I'm not going to have the kind of shop time I've had through the winter. Adding to that, Lovely Linda has a painfully long Honey-do list for me when nice weather settles in—endless yard and house jobs 1) I don't want to do and 2) are going to be in the way of shop work. You know the litany: "Honey, remember to fix the storm door. Honey, do you have the parts to fix the clothes washer? Honey, do what you can to fix that yard gate." I probably should have put my shop up in town so I wouldn't have it sitting there right in front of my eyes on days when I'm cleaning up the yard. The pain is almost too much.

Day 35 hours	2.0
Total project hours	121.0

Verification of the Truth of What I Say

The following two letters from Glenn Heideman don't offer much by way of technical advice—he's even more of a beginner than I am—but like this book, hopefully Glenn will give you heart that you are not alone in your trials and travails with your tractor (and probably in any other way for that matter). I read these letters and kept nodding my head and sighing and agreeing. I'll bet you do the same:

Roger,

Have just finished reading your book *Old Tractors*. How enjoyable. I am attempting to restore an Allis Chalmers D15, 1961 vintage. Your book really exposes many of my trials and tribulations with Allis. I am recently retired and purchased Allis for two reasons. My daughter and husband have an elk farm near here. Right—elk. Allis and I mow, blade, etc., on the farm. My second reason was for a winter project of restoration. Man, did I bite into a bucketful of bolts—rusty and greasy ones at that.

Allis arrived at the farm in September as the greasiest, dirtiest, mud-dauber infested tractor imaginable. No muffler, leaky manifold, leaky seals and gaskets just oozing oil and grease. Allis appeared to have not had a kind caress or pat on the hood for years. After the truck left, I hit the switch and Allis came to life. She wheezed, belched, fumed, spewed black smoke. I smiled as though being at the controls of Apollo 13. A look from daughter to father produced only a "Dad, I don't believe this" stare. Wife Elaine verbally: "Have you lost your mind?" expletive deleted. Granddaughter Maggie wanted to meet Allis and upon introduction said, "Cool, Grandpa. What is it?" Dropped my ego to -15 below.

As cooler weather was approaching, I needed a place to frolic with Allis. As we live in town and have but a two car garage, a decision had to be made. I have a 1956 Ford in mint condition that I like to stand back and admire. Either wife Elaine's car or the Ford had to set out. As neither car was agreeable to this suggestion, a storage garage had to be rented for the Ford. Wife Elaine to husband: "That storage costs more money . . . " expletive deleted.

By the way, I believe a garage is for parking vehicles, a shop is for working on them. We now have a "shoparage" attached to our home.

As a complete rookie at this venture, each turn of a bolt, each piece of metal removed, each fluid change is a challenge. Twisting a manifold bolt off in the head caused unbelievable dismay. After hours of frustration, consternation, and failure, the bolt finally submitted to the reality of "I am not really wanted here." There is enormous satisfaction in knowing that mind and matter can prevail over cold steel and red iron. This is my peak high so far. Peaks and valleys seem to be part of the territory, at least for this novice.

With minutes, hours, days, and weeks now turning into months, Allis is looking a little more like a lady than a tramp. So much so that she even got a new seat for Christmas. I expect that as she gets gussied up, even more good things will come forth— new muffler, new oil filter, a better rear tire, new gaskets and seals, new paint, and new decals. I believe Allis will appreciate a better way of life, at least she is in the shoparage nice and warm.

Finding parts and repairs is an adventure. This has taken me all over this end of the state and into Kansas. Why is it difficult to find number 12 orange wire? At first, I kept track of each purchase and shared them with Elaine. However, when the totals began to exceed a new front door for the house, a new shower stall for the bathroom . . . I began to rat-hole the receipts and now just grunt something inaudible like, "The big expenses are over, dear." "Fat chance," I hear someone say.

My shoparage really took on a new atmosphere when St. Nick left a new kerosene heater for it. Now I can scrape my knuckles, get extremely greasy hands, breathe too much dust, and utter completely unintelligible words and sentences in the comfort of a warm room.

Allis will be going to a body shop for a paint job somewhere between now and the next millennium. Then it will return for a final assembly, tune-up, admiring, bragging, and sweet talking. I sure hope she will perform as expected. Elaine has become involved with Allis and offers daily encouragement for the success of this project. She has accepted the fact that Allis will not come between us and our 43-years of marriage. I really appreciate that.

Again, your book rang so many bells and whistles that I felt compelled to relay my experiences so far. Thanks for writing about a subject that seems to grow and grow on those who understand or are beginning to understand the pleasures of working with old tractors.

Orangefully —Glenn Heideman

There are lots of important theoretical—if not theological—thoughts in that letter from Glenn but I would like to comment on just one. Surely you have seen the television situation comedy *Home Improvement* with Tim Allen. I cannot watch that show, which in every way seems to be a remarkably accurate reflection of life, without sputtering about this guy's utter idiocy in using as a shop, where he is presumably building a hot rod, an attached garage, with a door leading directly from his wife's kitchen into the shop area, where she also has her laundry appliances. Man, you'd have to be a raving idiot to have a shop attached to the kitchen, organized so there are regular visits from The Little Lady (or, if you are a female tractor mechanic with a non-tinkering husband, The Big Kahuna). Once, just to be funny, I mentioned that I might just put a small tool bench in the corner of our kitchen so I could clean parts and work on carburetors right up to supper time and during our evening television hours. Lovely Linda didn't get the humor.

Glenn, take it from me: nail up that door into the house, even if that means you now have to walk through the alley and back around the Hinky Dinky Supermart to get to your shop.

This is the next report from Glenn:

Roger,

Good things are beginning to happen to Allis. A winter in a warm shoparage has done wonders for both our attitudes. Those bitterly cold days afforded us a real opportunity to get right with it. Slowly—methodically!!—and sometimes painfully slow, parts and pieces are being put back in their places. As each was removed careful attention was given to where it came from—labels or tags to all—bolts, nuts, and washers carefully put into a can appropriately marked. Now, bolts and nuts have been cleaned with a soft wire wheel, threads cleaned and renewed, new washers applied—no expense spared or questioned here. Let's see—this bolt came from this hole—says so right here—why won't it fit? Drat.

Why won't the ammeter register anything—never did since the tractor arrived. First thought—generator not charging—wrong, checked out okay. Second thought—voltage regulator trouble, checked out okay. Third thought—ammeter defective—wrong, checked out okay. What's going on here? Time to look at the wiring diagram when all else fails. These color-coded wires must mean something, even to a novice like me. Let's see—brown wire goes from here to here, red wire goes from there to there, and so on. Whatdayaknow—the green wire is on the A field and the black wire is on the F field of the generator—reverse them and it registers all the way to 30. Wonder how many years Allis has had her wires crossed?

As fewer parts are now scattered about the shoparage and some semblance of order is being put into practice, the question from Wife Elaine remains, "What is the next big expense?" She heard someone muttering and gurgling about a paint job being the final LARGE expense. A "Fat chance, Bub" reply found my ears. An explanation stating that while there are more expenses likely to be made, some will be only slightly larger than others. Reply: "Ha."

The saga of Allis and a rookie continues. Grandson Nate: "Grandpa, maybe it is a real tractor after all!"

Orangefully—Glenn

Transmission Blues

I SPEND ALL MORNING TRYING TO mount the PTO transmission on the bottom of the main transmission, an awful long time for not much of a job. I go through a long series of trials and errors that always seem to be the case with me. The process reminds me that I am anything but an expert.

But I try. I cut a new gasket and apply a gasket sealer to the PTO case. I clean the six bolts and nuts and crawl under the tractor full of confidence. One stud extends from the transmission case, and that should make things easier. I can put the nut on that stud and it will hold the case in place while I fit the other bolts and nuts in place. Hmmm. Whoops. That works until I get to the two bolts at the rear of the case; apparently they have to fit around the shaft collar, and yet there really isn't enough room to slip the bolt heads past the collar. I try and try, but it doesn't work.

So I take the PTO case back off, covering myself with gasket sealer in the process. I pull off the collar so I can slip the bolt heads in before re-tightening it. I destroy the collar gasket, which means I have to cut a new one. Then I put the new gasket on and fit the bolts in the holes and . . . well, hmmm. That doesn't work either.

I go out to look at some other tractors and find that some of them don't have bolts at all. (If at all possible, you should have a tractor in running condition or know someone who does while you are working on a wreck, something you can refer to as an example now and then.)

Studs extend down from the main transmission case and nuts are turned onto the ends to hold the PTO case. No wonder I'm having trouble with *bolts*. I need studs. I cut studs from threaded stock, insert them into the main transmission case, re-seal the PTO case, and manage then to re-apply it to the main transmission. Just in time for lunch, I manage to complete this one, simple task. I need a plaque for my shop wall saying, "NOTHING'S SIMPLE."

In the afternoon I clean the interior of the implement lift gear box—a simple access to the drive shaft and its cover and put it together. (The Woodpecker has no implement lift on it, but the gear box and access port are still there.)

I turn my attention to the other end of the tractor. The crank on many Allis WCs extends through the cast-iron front pedestal and is permanently attached. That can be a convenience, but it is pretty vulnerable, sticking out there in front of everything else. Inevitably, you bump something with the front of the tractor—in this case, the crank—and it bends. The next time you try to turn the blasted thing, it won't. As I mentioned early on, the crank on The Woodpecker is bent, but good. I managed to get it out of the pedestal when I first started this project and I could see at once how it had been bent.

Now I roll it across a smooth surface again and mark the high spot. I put it in my shop press and apply a small amount of pressure, which improves the problem but doesn't solve it. I insert the crank back through the pedestal. When things are the way they're supposed to be, the crank just clears the steering sector, from which it picks up a small amount of heavy oil when it turns. That close clearance also means that even a slightly bent crank has a hard time clearing the sector. Again, I mark and bend. And again, and again, until eventually the crank turns easily and yet is still close to the sector so it can pick up that necessary oil.

Things are starting to fall into place, I tell myself—foolishly, as it turns out. I look for the next logical step in re-assembly. The shifter—that little box with the gearshift level sticking out the top and the gear forks out the bottom—seems a likely candidate. The Woodpecker's has a bent nail holding the reverse release latch in place and bits of wire holding the whole assembly together. The interior shows a little rust but is fairly clean and isn't rusted solid, which is a blessing. Maybe I'll get by without having to dismantle the whole thing.

The shift lever waves wildly from one side to the other, and that isn't good. The looseness means there is a lot of wear somewhere along the shifter lever, either on a little square pin that goes through the lever pedestal (or "tower"), or in the channel into which the pin fits, or somewhere down where the lever works in the forks and lugs that move gears around.

The gearshift lever comes out the top of the pedestal. I remove a spring clip at the top of the pedestal, a retainer ring, and the reverse release rod and the lever comes out. No doubt about it, it's the channel that is worn. I can see it. It's been beat to hell by that lever waving and slamming back and forth for 20 or 30 years, or maybe 40 or 50. It will have to be built up by welding or brazing.

Now I have another problem, too: the reverse release lever on the gearshift stick has a latch at its very end, near the bottom of the gearshift lever. It's still in the shifter case, above the shifter rods, and I can't get it out. At least I can't get it out without dismantling the shifter rods and forks. That's a complicated job. I decide to call it a day while I think over this predicament. It's supper time anyway.

Despite a slow start, it's been a good day, lots of little jobs finished.

Day 36 hours	6.0
Total project hours	127.0

Welding the Block!

WELSCH WEATHER REPORT

Another cold day but at least it's not rainy. Or snowy.

Since it's a Saturday, I think maybe Kenny Porath will come over and we can weld on the two cracked blocks sitting in the shop—the one that came off The Woodpecker and which I plan to re-install, and the spare one I would like to fix while we're at the task. Just before I go out of the house, Kenny calls and says he will be over right after he finishes a cup of coffee.

In the shop, I clean up a little, start a fire in the woodstove to warm the blocks to be welded, and figure while I'm waiting, I'll take another look at that shifter. I thought about the problem overnight. Last winter I spent a day with machinist Don Hochstetler learning about shifters. I got pretty good at dismantling them and putting them back together. I had some real confidence, and that was only a year ago. So I guess I'll take the shifter apart, clean it up, do it right, and use the exercise to remind myself how one does such things.

I cut the safety wires off the set bolts holding the shifter forks and lugs in place. I knock the end plugs out of the shifter case so I can slide the shifter rods out. I loosen the fork and lug on the first shaft and tap it carefully out of its place, taking care to catch the steel detent ball, spring, and "pill" catch that rides between the shifter rods to prevent inadvertent cross-shifting—getting into two gears at once. Everything goes smoothly.

Time flies by, but still no Kenny. I clean parts, consider the worn shifter lever, and am just about to clean up and go in for lunch, when Kenny drives in. He's ready to go, so I'll delay lunch until we've welded the blocks. What can that take? An hour?

Well, think again, Mr. Optimist. Six hours later we are still welding, grinding, drilling, brushing, welding, grinding, drilling, brushing . . . I've heard that welding cast-iron blocks is not an easy task, and now I see it first-hand. When we are finished—not to mention dirty, tired, and frustrated, the crack still isn't tight. The second block—the one I may need for The Woodpecker if the original doesn't work out—will have to wait. Unfortunately, so will the job of putting the engine back together—a major set-back in my schedule.

I close the shop with even more frustration because it may be weeks before I can came back out again and reconsider the problem of closing the gaps in the blocks.

Day 37 hours	6.0
Total project hours	133.0

Shifter Surgery

I'M NOT TOO EAGER TO TEAR INTO that shifter again, so I clean up a manifold, the one off the spare, back-up engine . . . and manage to break off two lugs. Two hours later I'm still drilling, tapping, cleaning up, and praying that I won't completely screw the casting and threads up. I get out of the mess relatively unscathed and decide maybe working on the shifter won't be as bad as I feared, considering. It's still where it was sitting when Kenny came over to weld the block.

I take out all the remaining rods, lugs, and forks, which is a lot bigger job than those few words make it sound. But it goes. I clean up the parts, and to my astonishment find that I have an extra "bullet"—the longish steel pellets that fit across the shifter rods and prevent the disaster of getting into two gears at once.

This can't be. An old timer I used to buy eggs from up in town always opened the egg boxes and counted, explaining, "Just want to be sure there's not an extra egg in there." These shifter parts are like eggs in an egg box: It's not possible to have extras. Yeah, I know that anytime you take something apart, you're likely to wind up with, uh, "extra parts," but not these. I stare at the assembly in utter bewilderment. Where the hell did that extra "bullet" come from?

It isn't until later that night that I come to the only conclusion I can imagine: sometime long ago, when someone else took this shifter apart, the bullet popped back into the compartment in the casting, *accessible only by popping out friction disks*. This guy didn't pop out the friction disks and therefore couldn't get the bullet out. His solution was to get another one and insert it into the shifter when he reassembled it, letting the lost one rattle around in the casting a few dozen years until I did pop out the friction disks and fished it out with a magnet. It's the only explanation I can imagine.

I give a try at brazing the knob end of the shifter lever and am surprised how smoothly the brazing metal flows into the worn groove. Boy, is it nice knowing I can do this. (Later, I also braze the "ears" onto an air cleaner base. Almost every Allis WC air cleaner I've seen has had the ears bent and torn, if not broken off; the discovery that I can actually *repair* them is a major victory for me.) I file the groove back into the shifter lever through the brazing. I make a new pin for the shifter tower and file it down until it fits comfortably in the hole. Hey, this mechanicking ain't so bad!

Re-assembling a shifter takes more arms than a normal man is issued at birth. All at the same time, you have to:

1) push on the shifter fork rod,

2) hold something into the casting at the opposite end to keep the detent ball and spring from popping back into the casting,

3) make sure the "bullets" don't slide out of place, and

4) push down on the ball.

All at the same time.

I put in the first rod, then remembering the shifter lug and fork need to go on first. So I dismantle it and start again. After going through this same routine three or four times, after several hours of agony, I get the thing back together. I have a scare when one of the lug set bolts gets crosswise and starts to cross thread in the fork base, but I stop in time and clean the threads with a chase. Finally everything is in place. I thread fine wire through the safety holes that keep the lug set bolts from accidentally unscrewing and falling into the transmission gears. I try it on the transmission. Everything works fine.

Wow! I did it! So I bolt the shifter back in place, a major leap in putting the ol' Woodpecker back together. I give the shifter another try. Oh Jeez. Something isn't working. The lever won't move. Then it moves too much. Oh no. The bottom ball has slipped out of the shifter lugs. That means there is still too much play between the lugs and the shifter lever ball. That means I should have built up the shifter lever ball as well as that pin channel. I have to dismantle the whole thing again and start over. A day's work—in large part for nothing.

Well, I can't really say that. I learned a lot today., and I had a good day in my shop with my tractor. I'll do the job again, and when I'm finished I'll know a lot more than I did when I started. I'll sure know better the next time!

In the remaining hour, I take on an easy task, cleaning the air cleaner, a matter of scraping off a lot of dirt and grease, rinsing out the bottom bowl, pulling out the coarse steel wool and rinsing off a half century of field dust, chaff, and bugs. I get that job done with no major disasters, and I stack the cleaned air cleaner at the other end of the shop along with all the other clean components that are piling up—timing gear cover, oil filter holder, head, wheel lugs, rods, pistons, cylinders, and oil pan. Once I get the block welded, I can re-assemble the engine, and I'll bet The Woodpecker looks like a tractor again. In the case of most of these components, now it's just a matter of bolting them back in place.

This has been a long, good day, despite the set-backs. I'm tired and content. Again, it's going to be a while—a couple weeks, probably—before I can get back in the shop, and when I do I'll have to face that blasted shifter. Well, I'm still looking forward to it.

Day 38 hours	7.0
Total project hours	140.0

Block Repair, Part II

I HAVE TAKEN A SERIOUS, REALISTIC look at what Kenny and I did by way of welding the cracked engine block, and it's not good. We welded too much at a time, causing the cast-iron to heat up and reject the weld, and where we didn't clean off "slag" carefully between weldings, there are pits and holes that go all the way through the block. I try rewelding them, but it just doesn't hold. Other cracks develop. The block was pretty well shot to begin with, but we have made matters worse.

I look at the spare block. I clean up its crack. Do I dare give it a try? Should I just use braze, or JB weld, or some other crack sealer? With the help of a first-class mechanic and welder I've managed to lose one block; could I possibly do better on my own?

This is another of those places where the delicate balance of respecting the machine while still appreciating that this is, after all, only a hobby comes into play. I don't want to screw up this block, not only because I want to do right by The Woodpecker but also because I want to be proud of my accomplishment; on the other hand, Rog, this is a piece of junk you started with, and if nothing ever comes of it, well, so what? Give it a shot, Rog. If you blow this block weld, most people will neither know nor care, and your pals who are following this project will be the first to understand; if you bring it off, well, you'll be something of a hero.

To make the story short, I clean the crack, groove it out slightly with a grinder, and weld it, this time using good nickel rod, warming the block thoroughly, welding very short lengths at a time, cleaning up the weld slag thoroughly between welds, tapping at the block to relieve stresses within the cast-iron, working slowly, carefully. By the end of the long, exhausting day, I am pretty satisfied, if I say so myself. The weld looks clean and tight. I can't spot any light coming through. The only true test, of course, will be when I fill the block with coolant, but I sure feel more confident about this effort than the previous one.

Day 39 hours	6.0
Total project hours	146.0

When an Engine Looks Like an Engine Again

FOR SOME REASON EVERYTHING is going right. (Probably because I am ignoring that crippled shifter!) The replacement block still looks pretty good to me. Time for the acid test—or perhaps better, water test. I put O-rings on the sleeves and push the sleeves down into the block, fill it with water, and . . . no leaks. I did it. I welded a block.

I figured I'd spend most of today drilling out the half dozen pan bolts that are broken off in the block, pretty much the same situation I had on the original block, which is now relegated to the scrap heap. This is not the kind of work I really enjoy, but I'm resolved to take my time with it and do it right. First I take a small round brush and clean the open bolt holes, using a chase to clean the threads. So far, so good. Then I kick myself because I should have cleaned up around the broken bolts when I first started working on this engine, putting drops of penetrating oil for the past three months, at least. But I didn't. So I start now.

First I decide to clean the holes as well as I can so the penetrating oil can get to the threads. I take a dental tool and start scraping . . . and whoops! The first "broken bolt" isn't a broken bolt at all; the hole is just full of hard, caked dirt. Ha! I clean out the hole, clean the threads with a chase, and move on to the next. At this point I have only four broken ones left, and I haven't even been here an hour. Hey, the second one is just caked dirt too. And the third, and the fourth, and the fifth! By late morning I am astonished to find that I have finished everything I planned for the whole day . . . no problems, no damage (to the block or me), no botched threads, no broken tools. I can't believe it.

Now what? Well, it seems like a big step, but . . . maybe I can start getting the crankshaft back in. Again, to my astonishment, everything goes smoothly. (Oh, please don't let this just be a major case of hubris, please!) The shaft is too tight when I finish; I can't turn the crank. I loosen the front bearing cap. The main shaft is still stuck. I loosen the back cap. Still stuck. It's the middle cap that needs a touch more give to it, obviously. So I cut some thin shims out of aluminum beer cans for the middle main bearing cap—a process that goes surprisingly easy—and slip them in between the cap and the block. I retorque the bolts and . . . Jeez, the engine turns smoothly.

As I eat lunch, I am in a state of shock. I'm almost afraid to go back out to the shop for fear a real disaster is yet to come. But I go, and I put in the pistons. Again, every goes with unreal smoothness. I have a little trouble getting one rod cap on . . . one of the bolts doesn't want to seat . . . but soon it falls in place too. I torque down the caps . . . and the shaft still turns smoothly, just a little more firmly, just as I would want it to do.

I go back to the house to clean up early. Linda and Antonia are surprised I am joining them early for supper, but they're no more surprised than I am. I try to tell them all the great things that happened, and while they try their best to appreciate talk of ring compressors, bearing shims, seals, "broken" oil pan bolts turning into caked dirt, and timing gears, it's just not their cup of tea. But they see how happy I am, and that's enough for them. It's sure enough for me. No sir, my friends, it really doesn't get better than this.

| Day 40 hours | 7.0 |
| Total project hours | 153.0 |

A Thread on the Web

Lee Klancher is not only the editor with whom I work at Motorbooks International but is also a friend. He's a nice guy, has a great sense of humor, likes machinery, and puts up with my crankiness. Can't find an editor much better than that. One of the things that baffles him, and several thousand other people I know from book publishers to my daughter Antonia, is that I have come so late to the Internet and World Wide Web. Until recently, I was darn near a Luddite about it.

Anyway, before I got online, Lee sent me a letter with his gentle arguments about how valuable a resource this computer terminal thing can be, and since it may be just the ticket for you, I include his brief note and a couple edited samples of the kind of thing that is going on out there in the world of electrons, bytes, bits, and old tractors.

Roger,

Rumor has it some fellow tried to convince you to get on the Internet. The guy sent me e-mail, wanting to know how to get in touch with you. Anyhow, I thought I'd show you a bit of what you are missing. The text below is what is known in net-speak as a thread. All that means is it is an ongoing conversation about a particular topic. The thread was started by a discussion of your book. The discussion that ensued—on torque wrenches—is still going on as of April 11. Kevin Cameron, one of my favorite motorcycle writers, recently called the Internet the 'CB radio of the 1990s.' Well put, I think. (By the way, "snail mail" is the U.S. Postal Service.)

—Lee Klancher

The first "correspondent" in the series Lee sent me commented on *Old Tractors and the Men Who Love Them* and that he liked it. He also mentioned me and my reluctance to get into electronic mail. The response to that entry seemed to kick things off in the direction of torque wrenches. In the book I write that I have and use torque wrenches but wonder if they are really all that necessary, since they weren't used by the farmers or mechanics who worked on these tractors in the first place.

Monday, 02 April 1996 12:05:31

Thanks for sharing this, Steve. I recently read his book and enjoyed it as well. One thing I noted was that he didn't seem to think there was much value in buying a torque wrench and torquing to specs. I was very close to buying a torque wrench before I read the book but now I'm not so sure. I would be curious to know what you and others on the list think about this.

—Max McF.

Wednesday, 03 April 1996 08:05:50

Max and others,

First, it's a matter of approach. To Roger, the idea of getting so involved, precise, and, well, anal about tightening nuts is completely counter to everything he is into antique tractors for. He is doing what he has to do and more power to him I say. But make no mistake about it: One day he will pay the price for not torquing nuts; and I am sure he understands that and is willing to pay it. Something will beg for a T-wrench and he will ignore it and the result will be either a leaking head gasket, slipping parts, cracked castings, something to be sure.

Basically, torquing with a T-wrench is imperative in a few circumstances, a real good idea in many circumstances, and unnecessary in most circumstances. If you read Roger's book, you will notice that he also does not get into real involved repairs: a little tinkering here, a little fiddling there. For example, if I remember correctly, you never see him tear down a transmission. The pinion shaft in the transmission of my Pacer calls for precise shimming and the nut on the end calls for 140 foot-pounds of torque. I would never install this shaft with[out] high quality shims, an accurate dial caliper, and a good torque wrench. I will not pretend that I know what 140 foot-pounds feels like. All of this shimming, measuring, torquing are completely counter to Roger's approach (an approach I share for the most part) but completely and 100 percent necessary. To reinstall the shaft without doing these things would be a good way to trash the $75 worth of bearings it rides on or worse.

It's all the approach, what's important to you, and what the trade-offs are. With a crawler, Max, I would have to believe a T-wrench is going to be a necessary evil for you. But it's up to you. Just realize that engineers don't devise unnecessary torque specs. They are there to save a part, ensure safety, maintain adjustment, bearing pre-load, you name it. Can you "do it by feel" most of the time? You bet. Just realize that one day will guess wrong—"This feels about right" even sound like famous last words—and it will matter and as long as you are willing to face that day I believe you are then making the right decision to forego the T-wrench. Good luck and sorry for getting long winded about it.

—Spencer Y.

Spencer was right about just about everything, as far as I can tell, except maybe that I do torque—just don't worship it—and I do tear down complete engines and transmissions and everything else—but I suspect there is a big difference between the number of torque specs in a Pacer transmission and an Allis WC transmission! In an Allis WC shop manual, no torque specs are cited for a WC gear box.

Wednesday, 03 April 96 10:52:39
Spencer,

No problem with message length. I recall that the last time I looked at T-wrenches at Sears there were at least two different types. One where there was a gauge at the end of the handle that measure foot pounds and another that had settings on a collar so that you could preset tension. What is the most reliable kind? Of course, I'm assuming a Sears T-wrench is an improvement on "this feels right." Maybe that's not a good assumption.

—Max McF.

Wednesday, 03 April 1996 11:30:29

I am not familiar enough with the workings to know if either [is] more accurate. Maybe someone can jump in here. I have used both kinds extensively. I love the audible kind (click when you hit the preset tension because it's fast, easy, and they stand up to tougher handling. I doubt they are necessarily any more accurate though and the settings are often too far apart. The only kind I still own is an old analog type where the bend of the shaft, relative to a separate pointer indicates force. These are the least accurate, but are much cheaper, and are reasonably accurate above 25 foot-pounds (do they still sell them???). I still have it because my Dad let me borrow the money to buy it and then never let me pay him back so I consider it a gift from him. It's a Craftsman and it's still going strong and holding zero 20 years later.

The pre-setable one was lost at a job site (used to test bolts on structural steel—it was huge—up to 500 foot-pounds and a three-foot bar. I have some nice scary stories from that job) and I have never felt compelled to replace it.

Either you feel comfortable with will be satisfactory. Just make sure it will handle up to 200 foot-pounds. I have never needed a micro torque wrench (0-25 or 50 foot-pounds) or anything over 140 foot-pounds. I mentioned for my small tractors. You probably have a few things on the crawler that could conceivably go to 175 or so. You may want to consult your service manual, scanning for torque specs.

—Spencer Y.

Man, there's a lot of good information there. Sounds to me like this Spencer is a good friend to know—very much like the guys I consult up at Eric's tavern on a regular basis.

Wednesday, 03 April 1996 09:20:17

The torque wrenches with the pointer dial are cheap but do a good job if you are careful when using them. You have to be careful that the pointer rod does not rub against the scale on the handle or your reading can be off. I have the pointer type as well as Sears top line clicker T-wrench. I really like the clicker type since it makes it easy to be consistent in the amount of torque applied to multiple bolts/nuts. It also makes it easy to pre-torque all the bolts to a lesser amount, then make a quick adjustment for the final pass at the specified setting.

—George B.

And another . . .

> Wednesday, 03 April 1996 09:29:33
>   I have one of those little ⅜ drive Snap-On T-wrenches. I picked it up at a garage sale and [it] is missing the guts to the head. What is the repair or return policy at Snap-On? I rarely see one of their trucks, mostly around here I see the MAC tool truck.

This "conversation" continues for many more days and pages and screens and contributors. In the intervening months since, the list has probably moved on to discussing shop calendars (Pamela Lee versus Cindy Crawford would make an interesting debate) or to building hydro-electric generators out of beer cans.

When I first read this "thread," I was working on The Woodpecker. I hadn't actually seen the image or process of the web on my computer screen. I didn't even have a modem, the little box that hooks a computer up to the telephone lines and, possibly, the Internet.

So what I mostly saw was people wasting way too much time and energy arguing about a $40 tool when they could have just bought the damned thing and gone to work in their shops. Grump, grump, grump, growl . . . .

In the ensuing year or so, I finished The Woodpecker, which is tucked safely under a tight roof. While I was doing the work I write about in these pages, I also learned how to weld . . . graduating from carbon arc torch to a stick welder, and finally to an oxyacetylene set-up. I even learned how to sandblast parts, and I learned more about the Internet.

A lot more.

As is so often the case these days, I was dragged out of the 20th century and into the 21st by my daughter, Antonia, and daughter-in-law, Beth. It was not a happy transition for me. I was perfectly happy with how my life was going and I could not imagine what good all this http, Gopher, www, Web, .com stuff could do for me.

But, well, we are so isolated out here in the Nebraska countryside and my daughter is an only child and, well, maybe there would be some good in it for her . . . so we bought a modem, contacted a local provider, installed some new software on my computer. . . and went on the Internet. That was six months ago and scarcely a day has passed when I haven't been at least impressed, more often astonished, at some new source, resource, listing, contact, or whatever for the average tractor nut. Yes, I have probably wasted far more time than I should have sitting here in front of this screen, but I have also found it a good and useful tool. Maybe you will too . . .

How do I feel about the Internet now? Well, why not stop by my home-page (http://www.micrord.com/rogerwelsch) and find out for yourself!

The Secret to Oil Pan Installation

WELSCH WEATHER REPORT

The year's bizarre weather continues: February was characterized with warm, balmy days, when I worked with my shop doors open. We are now into late May . . . but it's so cold, windy, and wet, I am building fires in the woodstove. That's okay. Warm days are great shop days in February, cool, rainy days are great shop days in May.

I HAVEN'T BEEN IN THE SHOP FOR many weeks, almost a month in fact. So I clean up the boxes and sacks of parts, rags, tools, etc., I've been tossing in the shop door for weeks. It's been so long I almost have to re-learn my way around the shop. There's a layer of dust on everything, including the tools on the work bench. Disgraceful. I'm surprised to see how far along the engine is. The tractor itself looks pretty much as it has for a half year—nothing but one frame rail, the rear end at one end and the front end at the other. But the engine is coming along. I turn it over on the stand and realize it really is time to start fastening things to it again.

Everything is pretty clean, so it's just a matter of putting on a gasket sealer and the gaskets and turning nuts and bolts. I attach the oil filter holder to the valve lifter cover. (I learned my lesson: Once before I put the lifter cover on the side of the block and then tried to attach the filter holder, only to find that the bolt heads for the holder were turning *inside* the cover and I had to take it off again! You have to put the oil filter holder on *first*.)

I bolt on the cleaned oil pump with no problem. Man, this is getting scary: it's time to close the bottom of the engine. That's always a heavy moment because you're closing up something you hope never to open again the rest of your life—something like a pharaoh must have felt when he sealed up a pyramid. I put gasket sealer on both the block and the pan and go in for lunch. I've found that if you rush this operation while the sealer is still soft, the gasket tends to slide around, or even pooch out between the components you're joining. Tacky sealer is a good glue, holding the gasket in place.

I'm impressed by how easy this job is this time. On every engine I have worked on before, I put the oil pan on while the engine was in place, attached to the frame rails and the transmission. That means I was lying under the thing on my back, trying to lift the pan into place, keeping the pan gaskets and thick crankshaft end gaskets all in place, pushing a pan bolt up into its home, and turning the wrench, all at the same time. I usually wind up with a distinctly bad disposition, along with hair shellacked with Form-a-Gasket. This time the engine is on a stand, about waist high, upside down. I can't believe how easy it is. I was uneasy about dismantling this engine and jerking it out of the tractor, but this one operation alone almost makes the whole thing worthwhile.

While the gasket sealer firms up, I clean the clutch. I recall how fearful I was when I first opened a clutch. Think about that: a clutch. That's got to be about the most complicated mechanical system I can imagine, even on something as elemental as an Allis Chalmers WC. (Remember, for me a door hinge is complicated.) Then I opened it, and there it was, a clutch, and it was about as obvious as . . . as . . . a door hinge.

That fear out of the way, I get to the process I like best in this mechanicking business—cleaning parts. By now you know I love taking filthy, black parts and making them shiny. For one thing, there's almost nothing I can screw up when I'm cleaning parts. I put good music on, sit at my bench, look out at the cold sheets of rain, and think how good life is. God, I do love this shop of mine!

The clutch goes together well. You have to understand when I say that, I don't mean there are no problems. I get the whole thing back together before I realize the drive shaft bearing needs to be in the flywheel before I close the clutch, so I have to take the clutch back off, install the bearing, and put it all back together again. Minor set backs like that are well within the parameters of "goes together well" in my book.

Day 41 hours	6.0
Total project hours	159.0

Cheap Therapy

**WELSCH
WEATHER
REPORT**

Yet another cold,
rainy day. The
weather is threat-
ening—lightning,
thunder, wind.
Now and then the
lights flicker in
the shop. I know
Linda and
Antonia would
rather have me in
the house to pro-
tect them from
the elements (!),
but . . . I keep my
eye on the out-
door thermome-
ter. At one point,
the temperature
falls in an hour
from 78 degrees
to 62. Tornado
weather.

AGAIN I HAVE ALL DAY TO ENJOY my shop. I tidy up the
rubble from a couple days ago, tighten down pan
bolts, look things over. The pan gasket is good and
solid. I turn the engine over on its stand and drag my
engine hoist over to The Woodpecker. That means I
have to clean up a lot of floor rubble too, just to get
the hoist in place. I clean a couple of engine head
lugs and install them so I can use the hoist. (I hoist
engines with a sling fastened to the head lugs.)

I lift the engine from the stand and detach it, the
first time it's been off those bolts for many months. I
lower it almost to the floor and support it on a couple
wood blocks, just about right for the clutch and flywheel, which I have put in place at its rear on a clean
towel. (Yeah, it's only the flywheel, but I worked hard
enough cleaning it up that I want to keep it clean.)

If I have done this job before, I don't recall, so I
wonder if I need to put the flywheel onto the crankshaft in any particular way. I look at the four bolt
holes in the flywheel and the crankshaft but don't get
any hints. I look through all my manuals and books.
Nothing about how the flywheel mounts on the shaft. So I push a bolt
through a hole and thread it loosely into the crankshaft end plate.

Hmmmm. The other holes don't line up. I unfasten the bolt and lay a
ruler across the holes. Now that I look more closely, two of the bolt
holes on the end of the drive shaft are closer to each other than the others. I should have known. The smart folks at the Allis Chalmers factory

engineered this thing so dopes like me *can't* put the flywheel on wrong, even 60 years later. I detach the flywheel, re-orient it so the holes match, and refasten it. Now it fits perfectly. I put the clutch parts back on the flywheel. I lift the engine with the hoist, push it over the remaining side rail, lower it, level it, push it back to the transmission housing.

Again, things go well, which is, again, not to say perfectly. I spend over an hour nudging, goosing, niggling, leveling, pushing, pulling, lifting, lowering . . . and all at once, there is a little jump, and the engine settles back against the transmission housing. The engine is back on ol' Woodpecker. The four bolt holes that mount the engine to the transmission housing are so perfectly (and accidentally, I should note) in line, it is only a matter of turning them into their holes.

Since only one side rail is in place, and therefore no front end support for the engine, I block it up with wooden blocks, but the fact of the matter is, the engine is back in place. This thing is beginning to look like a tractor again. It's nearly five o'clock and I promised Linda and Antonia I'd take them up to town for supper, so I have to leave everything pretty much the way it is. That's okay. I'm ready for a little celebration myself. I'll clean up when I come back.

While I'm turning off the lights and radio, covering up the solvents and kerosene containers, taking off my shop apron, cleaning the layers of dirt and grease from my hands, I can't help but admire The Woodpecker. I know she'd look like scrap iron to anyone else, but I remember what shape she was in when Jim Stromp hauled her here a year ago. I know what the engine looked like when I opened it up, and the transmission. Now it looks like a tractor again. A long weekend is coming up and Linda and Antonia will be out of town for a couple days. That means I'll be back out here in the shop soon. Hot dog. I may make my deadline of September, a mere three and a half months away now.

Of course it doesn't matter. As much fun as I'm having with this project, I'm sure not going to act like it's a job.

Day 42 hours	6.0
Total project hours	165.0
(I wonder what rich folks pay for 165 hours of psychological counseling and therapy? A lot more than I've spent for parts, I'll bet.)	

Restorer Accounting

I REPLACE THE SECOND SIDE RAIL once the engine is in place and start to put bits and pieces back on the engine block—oil fittings, water pump, crank pulley. I flush the radiator, which is badly battered on the outside but seems to be tight. I can't believe how much dirt comes out of the cooling fins on the exterior of the radiator—the legacy of the machine's long residence in a remote wood lot.

It's clear I'm going to have to buy some soldering equipment and learn a little about that craft before I can repair the radiator and remount it to the frame rails. That will set me back a while because I have nothing by way of soldering tools and know nothing about the process.

One could legitimately argue the economics of this decision: I could take this radiator to a shop specializing in exactly this problem and for a hundred bucks or less get a first-rate job done on it, and be through the problem. But to me it is obvious that would be exactly the wrong thing to do: I am interested in process, learning how to do these things, going through the job, wrestling with the problems, solving them on my own. When it comes right down to it, the radiator isn't the point at all; it's repairing the radiator that matters to me, and even more than that, it's me repairing the radiator that matters.

The other course of action, after all, carries with it the very clear extension of logic, why do any of this? Why not let someone else do the whole thing? Why bother doing any of this, or learning any of the skills? Then it becomes even more clear that actually it's not even me repairing the radiator that matters—it's me learning how to repair radiators. I imagine if I really got serious about this, it isn't even a matter of learning how to repair a radiator but simply keeping my mind active by learning.

(Okay, okay, okay . . . there will almost certainly be a few of you who see through that explanation and know that the bottom line: What I'm working up to here is going to a couple of shops and buying new tools. Yeah, that's what it's really about—NEW TOOLS! Now that I've convinced myself that I have to buy them, I can get on with the tasks I can complete with the tools I already own.)

I cleaned the block some time ago, and the rocker arms, valves, and valve lifters. Everything seemed to be in fair condition at the time, but now that I look things over, I notice that the valve seats in the head are badly pitted. For the kind of performance I expect from this engine, I tell myself, a little pitting shouldn't hurt anything. But then I think again, and tell myself, Welsch, if you're going to do this, do it right. So, I take another look at the valve seats.

They are damaged beyond the kind of repair I can do with a little, simple "lapping in" of the valves with a hand rod and some valve grinding compound. I can see that clearly now, and I have to admit it. I ask around up in town about how one handles a situation like this. Friends knowledgeable about mechanics tell me that the thing to do is to haul the head to a *real* machine shop (Jeez, I hate the way they say that!) and have the seats reground. Tonight I'll look up "valve seat grinder" in an old Snap-On tool catalog I keep by the bed—first, to see what a valve seat grinder looks like, and secondly, to get an idea what one costs.

By looking at the basic tool and its adjuncts, it becomes quite clear how it works. The price list makes it clear—vividly clear—that there is no way in hell I'll ever afford one. What I do is take the Snap-On price, cut it in half, and figure that's about what a new machine would cost elsewhere. Sure, I'd like to own a set of Snap-On tools, but I know just as surely as my name is Roger "Low-Budget" Welsch, I'll never buy more than an occasional, small item from Snap-On. I ask Al Schmitt up at the town's service station to check on some prices for me from other suppliers, and his report is not encouraging.

Conclusion: I'm not going to get a new valve seat grinder.

Next, I advertise in some local newspapers and get some bids closer to my economics—$600, $500 . . . probably fair prices for good machines—mostly Sioux. Finally I get a nice letter from a fellow not far from here who has pretty much what I think I need. Linda, Antonia, and I go to a movie in the town where this man lives and drop by to look at his machine. It is clean, runs well, has a diamond-base stone truer, and a couple extra grindstones and spindles. I wind up with what I need for $150—not a cheap tool but better than the thousands of dollars a new machine would have cost.

I am delighted when I set up the shop the next day and grind the valve seats in two heads slick as a whistle in a matter of minutes. What's more, the grinder will probably be worth even more 20 years from now when I finally sell off my shop, so, I tell myself, "Think of it as an investment, Rog."

Back to where I started: I look at the pitted valve seats and decide I can't go much further, so I spend the rest of the afternoon cleaning up in the shop, getting ready for brother-in-law Steve to pour a new floor in my parts bay and outdoor work bay. I've found that blowing dust, snow, and weeds make a real mess of my parts shelves in the open shed built onto my shop, so I'm going to pour cement and put in sliding doors across the open end. Which means I have to take out all the parts that are already stored there. That's a mountain of moving.

Also attached to the shop has been an open-wall shed with an overhead hoist for pulling engines and transmissions. I thought it would be great to work out here in the summer when it's too hot in the shop, but the dirt floor makes work impossibly dirty. So, we're going to cement it too, while we're at it. That means I've got to move the three tractors out that have been sitting in that bay for a year or so. Whew.

Day 43 hours	3.0
Total project hours	168.0

DAY 44

Manifold Disasters

THE DAY TURNS INTO A DISASTER. Actually, things go well for a while. Now that the valve seats are clean and smooth, I quickly re-install the valves and rockers and put the head on the block with a new gasket. Terrific. Now the engine is starting to fall into place.

I find that the shifter pedestal still isn't right. When I move the shifter lever around, the little ball on the end of the rod finds its way out of the shifter rod lugs, which means I might be driving along some day on this machine and try to take it out of gear—with no luck. Or, two gears might slam into the wrong slots and shell out the entire interior of the transmission. The little ball on the end of the shifter lever needs to be built up with brazing metal (I brazed the slot on the end but haven't done anything with the larger ball), and then ground and filed to size again. It's not an impossible job, but it's a biggie. I'll set it aside and take on the task another day, maybe when I've had a little more experience brazing.

The rest of the day I sit quietly at my work bench, cleaning up the manifold, which goes well. I do a particularly good job and am, I'll admit, darn near smug about how things move along. I make new studs for the manifold and dig out some pretty, shiny brass nuts to mount it. I put new gaskets on the manifold and move it carefully into place. Wow, is that pretty, or what?! I tighten down the nuts and she looks great.

Just one more snug-up on each of the manifold nuts and . . . *ah shit!!!* A little ear on the manifold casting snaps off! The cleaned, manicured manifold is *broken!* Damn, damn, triple damn. Utterly dismayed I drag out another manifold and mount it in place of the broken one. In order to salvage something from this major disaster, I decide to practice my brazing, and I braze the ear back in place on the manifold. Will it hold? It looks good but I just don't know. I'll try it somewhere down the line when I finally get my test engine set up on a stand outside somewhere.

Fairly well disheartened, I close down the shop for the last time in a long time. Now I really have to get busy cleaning the parts and tractors out of what will be my parts room. I'll try to find some time to learn how to solder. I have a mountain of work to get out of the way before I can get back to The Woodpecker. I close the door with a heavy heart.

Day 44 hours	4.0
Total project hours	172.0

More Webfoots

At some point I wrote to my cousin Jim Glenn about this whole computer terminal thing. Sometime in the past he mentioned that he dabbles in it and that there is some information about tractors I might find interesting or useful or both. So, I wrote him again and asked him to send me some samples of the kinds of things he finds and retrieves for his youth, which he generously did.

No doubt about it, for someone who is serious about this tractor thing, for someone who is looking for information, tools, data . . . the Web opens up a whole new world. Jim used the YAHOO! search engine, which is actually a whole lot easier to work on than a WC.

The variety of information available at the click of a mouse is staggering. There is a list of sites for old stuff—antique music boxes, pick-up trucks, automotive events, motorboats, fire trucks, motorcycles, street rods, and a weekly story about life on the farm and information on antique farm tractors. I'm already worn out.

The specific lists Jim called up are: "Ageless Iron," information and articles from the wonderful *Successful Farming* series dreamed up and nursed along by Dave Mowitz, tireless editor of that magazine—a bunch of my stuff shows up here; Antique Mechanics, a body of information drawn from the University of California's Davis Campus Antique Technology Collection—with pictures of the tractors in question; and even more impressive, Yesterday's Tractors, 16 pages of classified ads for tractor stuff—everything from T-shirts and books and manuals to videos, toys, and enameled signs. Perhaps most impressive was the 16—16—pages of classified ads under "new and used tractor parts"—equipment, parts, help-wanted, clubs, tires, everything you can imagine, right up to and including entire tractors!

This is exactly the kind of testimony that pushed me onto the Internet. Who knows, it may do the same for you!

Radiator Surgery

AFTER SIX WEEKS OF WORKING AT OTHER tasks, pouring the cement floor, sorting and restocking parts, hauling tractors in and out, looking longingly toward the locked up shop, I am back. There are a couple dead birds on the floor—they must have gotten in somewhere and couldn't get out. Things are tidier than I remember. The Woodpecker waits patiently, just as I left her. Inside the door there is a pile of rags, supplies, tools, coffee cans, paper towels, and other things I've picked up or brought back over the past couple months and tossed inside the door to be sorted later. This is, I guess, later.

I spend the day putting things away, sweeping the floor, looking things over. I remember that the next step in the progression was the radiator, and that I had planned to learn to solder so I could fix up The Woodpecker's battered coolant system. I guess now's the time, even though it's hot enough that the lead may be molten before I heat up the iron.

I look at the radiator. The sheet metal cowling has broken loose, and I can see that it was originally soldered. The metal is torn in a few places too. With pliers I spend some time bending and forming the thin metal plates back to a rough semblance of what they looked like before they were tortured out of place.

I take a quick glance at the chapter on soldering in my welding manual; I don't need much review because even though I haven't been in the shop working for a long time, I *have* spent hours before going to sleep looking through my books and manuals. After a few false starts—I find the soldering iron doesn't work nearly as well on big jobs like this as a torch does, precisely as the welding manual suggests, and the book is also right (really right!) about the necessity of cleaning the metal well before trying to solder—things start to go better and pretty soon I have to admire my progress.

Somewhere in my turning of the radiator this way and that, some twigs fall out of the filler vent. That's not uncommon. A tractor sitting out in the rain and trees for decades provides lots of opportunities for critters of all kinds—birds, mice, bugs, squirrels—to build new homes in snug, dry places. So, tool boxes, manifolds, crankcases, even radiators get full of twigs, mud, feathers, leaves, hulls, whatever. In this case, it was the radiator and it was full of twigs.

I pull out all that I can with needle-nose pliers and haul the radiator outside to flush it again, a little confused because I'm sure I already did that once and surely some of these sticks should have come out then. But . . . anyway. So, I start running water through. It doesn't come out as fast as it goes in. Not nearly as fast. Sticks, dirt, grass, all sorts of trash wash out, and water still has a hard time coming through. I try putting some pressure on the input by holding my hand firmly around the input hole (actually the exhaust hole at the bottom of the radiator, but you know what I mean), and out comes more dreck. The water is still sluggish.

More dirt and sticks come out, uh oh . . . water springs out of various holes and the holes get bigger as the mud gets thicker. Efforts to force water through the radiator simply reveals more leaks. So, I see I have two problems with this radiator, and they are big ones: 1) it is severely clogged and is going to take a lot of additional work to be clear, and 2) it has a lot of leaks that will take more than a chemical sealant to close up.

On one hand, this is precisely the kind of thing I enjoy in tractor restoration, a chance to learn something new and deal with new problems; on the other, I would like to get The Woodpecker up and running and I do have five or six spare radiators I have taken off spare parts tractors. Begrudgingly admitting a minor defeat, I take the leaky, clogged radiator back to the parts room and tuck it away, figuring I'll spend some quiet, snowy day another winter working on it. (Next time I'm in town, I'll ask some questions about what I should use to flush out a thoroughly clogged radiator.)

I take a spare radiator out to the yard and run some water through it. It seems to be in pretty good shape, so maybe . . . whoops—all at once a long slit of water gushes from the entire bottom of the radiator. The bottom reservoir is split, stem to stern. Water probably trickled into it during the years, froze, and split it. Another job for a long winter's day. I drag it back to the parts shed and grab another. Its sheet

metal is pretty shaggy, bent, torn, broken from the core, but since I
fixed that sort of problem on the original radiator, I can probably do it
again on this one.

I start out to the yard . . . and I can see a split in its bottom in exactly
the same place as the last one. Damn. Back to the parts shed. There are
two radiators left. One is from a styled WC. The Woodpecker is unstyled.
That means I have one radiator left. (That's not really a problem.) I plan
to dismantle two or three more tractors for parts before winter sets in, so
I'll have a few more chances for a decent radiator, but I sure would like to
solve this problem now.)

I take the last survivor out to the yard and look it over. Hmmm. It really is the best of the lot so far. Not too badly beat up—a few bent fins, a
little sheet metal damage. I run water through it. It flushes freely, cleanly, with no leaks. Jeez, this one is almost too good for The Woodpecker!
I take the radiator into the shop, dismantle it insofar as one can dismantle a radiator, clean out the ports and fittings, cut and scrape off old hose
and fittings, solder loose ends, run a thread chase through the mounting
holes, and carry it to the front of the tractor.

Now, I'm rolling and it's time to quit. Next time I get into the shop, I'll
mount the radiator and install new hoses and clamps. I can hardly wait.

Day 45 hours	5.0
Total project hours	177.0

Transmission Transfusion

Another long, endless spell without time to get to the shop—almost a month. But I couldn't have chosen a better day—the earliest snow in history—cold, icy, and not even the end of September! Thing is, it's winter again, and this is the second winter for The Woodpecker in the shop. I was supposed to have the tractor finished and the rechristening party over by this time.

I START BY PUTTING THE STEERING SHAFT and wheel back together—a fairly simple process. I drain the kerosene out of one of the final drives and fill it with heavy gear oil, and I turn again to the shifter assembly that has been haunting me for months. All the parts—most of them anyway—are in a bucket along with a couple dozen dead crickets. I look everything over and try to remember the situation. Somewhere along the line I brazed the end knob on the shifter lever, but now it won't fit in the shifting lugs, so I must not have ground it down; the stabilizing lug in the shifter tower—a notoriously weak element in Allis Chalmers tractors—is shot, and I had ground a new one out of a bolt, but I must not have finished grinding it down, either. It needs more work, too.

I grind down the tower lug and shifter knob and manage to fit the whole assembly together yet once again, only occasionally losing detent balls and springs. Then I run smack into my lack of expertise (and into the problems that inevitably result from long absences from the shop.) I go through the elaborate and strenuous process of inserting a shifter rod into the shifter casing, slipping the springs and balls in place, and then, it hits me. I forgot to put the shifter lugs and forks on the rod beforehand, which means I have to take the whole thing apart again, put on the lug and fork, and repeat everything from scratch. I don't even want to consider how many times I've taken this apart and put it back together again now.

I remember to put the lug and fork on the next shifter rod before inserting it (there are three rods) but find I've put the fork on backward, and so once again I take everything apart and put it back together again. Now, there's nothing unusual about all this so far because this is the way things go for me (and, I suspect, for a lot of amateur mechanics). I remind myself I do this to relax and what the heck, I'm just getting plenty of practice at what I need to know anyway.

Now I find that the end ball of the shifter lever is still loose and slips through the lugs with distressing ease. I peer into the shifter mechanism and see that the middle shifter lug is badly worn; it won't do any good to braze more on the shifter lever because then it won't accept some of the other parts that need to be slipped on it. Do I braze and fill on that worn shifter lug? Well, I should but that would involve dismantling the whole shifter again. And how much should I build up the worn shifter? I have no idea what a new one looks like!

I drift out to the addition on my shop where I store parts. There's an old, broken shifter lying there on a shelf. I drag it into the shop and take a look at it. It's a mess. The casing is badly cracked—unrepairable. So I dismantle it completely. I clean the detent balls and springs, shifter rods, forks, lugs, rings, and washers. To my utter amazement, I find that I'm not the first one who's grubbed around in there! Someone must have tried to repair this mess another time, maybe giving up and deciding the whole damned tractor wasn't worth saving. Anyway, right there on the middle shifter rod is . . . a brand-new, pristine, virgin shifting lug . . . exactly the part I need, and only the part I need.

Now I have another dilemma. I could insert this new part in The Woodpecker and be pretty much done with my shifter problems. But I was dealing with another problem when I got to this point: What does a new lug look like? Figuring if I had an answer, I could repair the worn lug, and other worn lugs for the next 10 or 20 years. In other words, should I go the simple route of using the part or go the long way and use it as a model?

Remember? I am doing this for the fun of the process. The less process, the less fun. Wouldn't it be great if I had a entire Allis WC that was entirely new?! Then I'd know what everything should look like. In the meanwhile, I'll take this one little step. I dismantle the entire shifter and put the worn lug and new lug on my welding table. I go happy, through heavy September snow, back to the house. Next time I get out to the shop, I will play with brazing that lug. If it doesn't work, hey, I got a brand new lug to work with anyway! Is this some kind of life or what?!

Day 46 hours	5.0
Total project hours	182.0

Burnt Flesh and Bolting Back Wheels

I'VE BEEN WRESTLING A FEW MONTHS with a murderous work schedule, so my contact with the shop consists mostly of drifting by its doors as I drive in and out of the yard. I look wistfully in its direction and sigh. I did get Antonia, my daughter, to help me drag another parts tractor into the dismantling bay so I can work on it during the nice days of the approaching winter. I hauled an engine into the shop, hoping that this winter I can fulfill a long dream of mine, to rework, rebuild, polish an Allis WC engine until it is as good as I can get it. I want to put it on a portable mount, a sled of some sort, so I can slide it in and out of the shop. Something of a power unit, a test stand engine . . . yep, just like I wanted to do last winter.

I would like to ask my mechanic buddies to help me get this engine into superb running condition. Then, say I have a carburetor I'm not sure of. I'd take the carb off my test engine and put the questionable one on. Technically, the only variable on that engine should be the carb. As it is, I'm never sure whether I'm working with a bad fuel system, faulty magneto, clogged carb, stuck float, bad plugs, whatever.

What? I already told you that? Well, it's been a long project, this Woodpecker thing, and I tend to drift a little as I get older.

Today is warmer than usual for the season—winter is moving in and we've had our first good snow—so I throw open the door and sweep things out, haul out scrap metal and garbage, generally put things into order. It's not really tractor work, but it's the kind of thing that's necessary, not only for the shop but for the soul. In the little time I have today, I remount the gas tank supports and gas tank. (I better test out that fuel system some time soon, while I can still have gas dripping without worrying about a hot wood stove. Bad combination!)

Then I decide it's time to put the back wheels back on—at least working wheels I can use to get The Woodpecker back out of the shop and maybe running. So, I roll two steel-lugged wheels into the shop, which is not an easy task. In fact, I can't imagine anything more clumsy. They must weigh a quarter ton, and if one of them gets a little out of balance while you're rolling it, you're going to lose it, and God help whatever's under it.

I do all right with the first wheel, and just about have the second wheel in place when it starts to lean a little too far. I put out my hand to keep myself and the wheel from falling . . . and put that hand directly onto the red-hot woodstove. The timing is perfect because I'm just recovering from a good burn I got while doing some welding. Damn.

Now comes the frustration of trying to maneuver the wheels into position—with one badly burned hand, on top of everything else. There are probably some secrets old-timers know about this process, but they sure have escaped me. Thing is, you have to bring the rear axle to just the right height. Then you roll the iron wheel into place. You can count on the holes of the wheel not matching up with the lugs on the tractor. They never do. You can't spin that wheel, so you try to turn the axle. But you have to have the axle steady when you start to lever that wheel into place, so you set the brakes. Inevitably, as you move the wheel, it is no longer in line. But you can't move the hub any more because you've set the brakes. If this doesn't sound frustrating to you, read it again, and add your own details. It's murder.

At any rate, I do get both back wheels on The Woodpecker with no additional injuries. I'm exhausted and hurting, but I still have an hour in the shop, and it's been so long since I've had an hour here, I figure I better use it up, tired or not. I put on the air cleaner. Wow. It looks even more like a tractor now!

Day 47 hours	5.0
Total project hours	187.0

A Newbie's Guide to Plowing the Internet

I don't want for a moment to suggest that I know what I'm doing when it comes to the Internet. I'm just a beginner when it comes to tractor restoration . . . but I am nothing but a babe when it comes to Web surfing.

Even at this elementary stage, however, the potential of this enormous connection with the world is obvious to me. This electronic monster is continuously in flux, with new material and sites being added, old ones dying away, and quality improving and dropping. Anything I can tell you now is almost certainly going to be out-of-date by the time this book sees print. I am going to show you a modest, hopelessly incomplete list of what I found with just an hour's worth of looking around for addresses. No matter what you're looking for—information about an obscure tractor part, a source for odd tools, information about a type of magneto long out of production, books, friends—it's all there somewhere on the Internet, believe me.

In case you're not at all familiar with what the Internet is, it is simply a network of computers, big and small, connected together. It really is "world wide." Not long ago, I sent a letter by post office to a soldier in Saudia Arabia; days later, he responded . . . by way of my computer screen. If there's a problem, it's that there is so much information available that you can scarcely sort through it all. It's a matter of taking a few hours, a half day, or even a whole day, and "surfing" . . . clicking and pointing and looking and choosing . . . and finding whatever suits your fancy.

A good place to start is with "search engines" and "link" sites. Search engines are simply services that help you find things. They ask you what you want, you type in "antique tractors," and the engine goes to work to the 1,000 . . . or 10,000 . . . places it thinks you might find what you need. Then you can try another search engine and see what it comes up with for you.

Link sites are places where some kind soul has gone through the trouble of saving you a lot of work. He or she has found everything that relates, in our case, to antique tractors. You "visit" their link site, look at the titles, and maybe summaries of what they have found, and then, with a click of a button, you can visit the sites that interest you. A really nice link site for us old tractor nuts is Tractorworks or Tractorlinks (see addresses below).

Other places allow you to put your name on a list and join an ongoing conversation about a particular topic (as shown in "A Thread on the Web"). There are sites where someone tells you what they're doing with their tractors and how they're coming along . . . and parts sources . . . and

funny stuff . . . and club news . . . and information about upcoming
machinery show . . . and, well, you get the idea.

Rog's Favorite Web Sites

Adept Resources Fastrac Home Page
http://www.adeptr.simplenet.com

Ageless Iron
http://www.agriculture.com/contents/sf/ageless/agiindex.html

Antique Mechanics Home Page
http://www.ece.ucdavis.edu/~hulse/index.html

Antique Power
http://www.antiquepower.com

Antique Tractors
http://www.fastfinder.com/antiquemachinery.html

Antique Tractors
http://www.vaxxine.com/stuard/jd.html

A.T.I.S. Home Page
http://website.informs.com/ATIS

Best of the Rest: Antique Tractors
http://www.eagles.usit.net/trctor/Best/Best.html

Binder Books
http://www.binderbooks.com

Classic Tractor Playing Cards and Collectibles
http://www.classictractors.com/

Farmall Page
http://www.student.toplinks.com/hp//eo/index.html

Machinery Forum
http://www.farmshow.net/chat/machinery/

Massey-Harris
http://www.m-h.cs.uoque/hp.ca

Motorbooks International Home Page
http://www2.motorbooks.com

Museum Net: Links to Other Agricultural and Farm Machinery Pages
http://www.lookup.com/homepages/79116/links.html

Official Roger Welsch Homepage
http://www.micrord.com/rogerwelsch

Rumely Oil Pull Page
http://www.chem-eng.toronto.edu/~dorset/

Stephen Equipment's Antique Farm Machinery
http://www.users.aol.com/glaq/antigue.html

Surplus Tractor Parts
http://www.stpc.com

The Old Farm Tractor Source
http://www.iupui.edu/~harrold/javascript

Tractor Blue Book
http://www.farmequipmentguide.com

Tractorville USA
http://www.geocities.com/Heartland/8367

Unofficial Allis-Chalmers Page
http://www.dstratton.com/allis/index.html

Unofficial Minneapolis-Moline Page
http://www.netbci.com/users

Yesterday's Tractors
http://www.olympus.net/tractors

Drop me a line if you know of any others—
that's captnebr@micrord.com

Front End Transplant

THE BACK WHEELS ARE NOW ON, and maybe I should consider the fronts. Tires are perhaps the biggest problem I have with my tractor work. I rarely find a tractor with tires in any kind of usable condition. I haven't located a source of used tires in the sizes I need, haven't come up with suitable substitutes, and new tires are fiercely expensive, too rich for my budget. I don't need much by way of rubber. Tractors like The Woodpecker will probably never travel more than 10 miles the entire rest of their lives and certainly never work under strain.

I've dismantled about 16 tractors for parts now, and whenever I can, I pick up tires and wheels at sales or junkyards. The accepted pattern is usually you find exactly what you need a week or so after you went ahead and bought the same thing for a lot more money somewhere else. So, since it's a nice day, I take a walk around behind my sheds and take inventory. I find two matched front tires in fair condition. I'm a little surprised and very pleased with this turn of events. But then something occurs to me: some Allis WCs have front hubs with five lugs, some with six. The wheels have five lug holes. I check in the shop—yep, The Woodpecker hubs have six. The tires are in fair condition, but I don't think they'll handle being taken off these wheels and put on others. Ouch. Something of a set-back.

Now I have another decision to make. I take another look at my tires and wheels and decide I could:

1. Spend some money, buy new tires, and put them on six lug wheels.

2. Change the hubs on The Woodpecker, putting on five-luggers—and that's a real option because changing hubs is not all that tough a job. I check around the yard and find a front end with a pair of good, five-lug hubs. In fact, I even have some clean, five-lug hubs on my parts shelves.

3. I could drop the entire front-axle assembly out of the front pedestal and slip a new one in—maybe even the one I found outside with the two good hubs already on it.

As I think about the options, I lean toward the last. Thing is, I have gone through The Woodpecker putting just about everything into good condition—except that front axle assembly and the hubs. They feel firm and roll smoothly, so I just presume the bearings and seals are okay. But that isn't the way I want to do this job; I want to do it right. Maybe this, then, is a good place to pick up that little piece of rebuilding I missed.

My own preference is to keep as much as the original iron on a tractor as possible when I rebuild it. No particular reason, I just like to save as much of what was there as I can. I'm not a perfectly-accurate-restoration nut. Sooner or later, you're going to run into one of these guys. They know each and every minute detail of a tractor, right down to the kind of spark plug wire originally issued with your machine. You know the type: "Hey, boy . . . you got a number three grade bolt on that tool box. You know, from serial number 342,550 tractor manufactured in June of 1931 to number 377,237 made April 15, 1933, used a number two carriage bolt produced in the Birmingham plant of Atlantic steel, except for just a couple that were turned out on January 4th, when a guy named Goober McNally in the front office forgot to order the bolts and they borrowed some from a stove manufacturer just down the street. In that case, the bolts in question are . . . " You get the idea.

That's fine. I admire that kind of obsessive behavior. I even understand it, sort of. Thing is, I don't share it. I do what I can to keep my tractor looking like an Allis WC. I don't put on anything that is clearly out of place—like a John Deere air cleaner. I don't weld on dumb stuff like hood ornaments. But I don't get carried away. I try not to do any permanent damage. I know the webbing I put under my gas tanks is not precisely the same kind that came out on the Allis originally, and frankly I don't care. I know the tires I'm going to wind up putting on The Woodpecker are not the original diamond-tread pattern. So what? If it's such a big deal, when some anal-retentive restoration nut winds up with this tractor, *he* can "do it right." Me, I do what I can. After all, which is *really* the most accurate? An Allis with a precisely accurate rear PTO mount, just as it came off the assembly line, or one with an old Model-T Ford running board bolted across the back fenders and PTO mount, just like 10,000 farmers did it from one end of the country to the other? They are both accurate representations of two different things.

So, I order new tires for the front end, without worrying about accuracy. I spend the day removing the front axle assembly from the front end in the yard, disassembling it, thoroughly cleaning it, replacing bad seals. The bearings are a little loose but not bad. The wear isn't too bad. It has some little peculiarities (some kind of stalk shield bolted on the front, an extra set-screw fitting welded onto its body) but when I'm done, I'm pleased with what I have.

So that's it, then: I'll drop the front axle assembly out of The Woodpecker's steering pedestal and slip this one in. Tomorrow. Now things are rolling along.

Day 48 hours	4.0
Total project hours	191.0

Sex and Sledge Mauls

I JACK THE WOODPECKER'S FRONT end up off its blocks, put two longer blocks under the front engine mount, remove the previous front blocks and lower the tractor down on these new, further-back blocks, so the front end now hangs free, where I can work on it. I turn the large bolt holding the axle assembly to the vertical pedestal's steering post and remove the set screw that holds it there. Nothing.

Hmmm. I think the axle assembly is supposed to slide right off. The other one came right off the pedestal out in the yard. I just pulled it up and off it came, slick as can be. I check my tech manuals. No indications of any hidden snap rings, set screws or pins. I tap at the assembly tentatively with a hammer. Nothing. I pry at it a bit. Still nothing. I bang at it real well. Still nothing major.

There is the slightest movement, I think. I bang a little more. Now I have maybe a 16th of an inch. I just hope I'm not getting this movement by boogering up something inside the pedestal. I bang a little more. No, the assembly is moving, ever so slightly, but the steering post is staying put, just as it should. I get a bigger maul and pound a little harder. There is movement but not very blasted much. Still, movement is movement.

As it turns out, I wind up spending almost two hours banging and prying, and then, as such things often happen, it finally gives up and slides smoothly off the post. Apparently, the only problem was a slightly banged up keeper key that holds the assembly from turning on the post. The end of the key is bunged up, so maybe that was it. It doesn't matter any more. The axle is off and everything seems to be in good shape, so it can go on the parts shelf.

I have pretty much used up the afternoon—and any energy I had—banging away at that stuck assembly, but since afternoons have been coming along so few and far between, maybe I should try to do at least one more thing. Put the new assembly on? After what I just went through, that seems like a pretty big project for so little time.

I take the new axle component over to the front end, grease it up good, and use a hydraulic floor jack to ease it up into position. It slips easily into position. I tighten down the big bolt holding the assembly in place and tighten the set screw. I can't believe it. It took five minutes, and it's done. It looks great. It has about the right amount of play and feels firm. The front end is solid, the bearings and seals are good, and, for whatever reasons, I wound up doing the job right.

I still have an hour. I'm going to do something fun for that hour. I spend a little time taking the head off my winter-project engine and scraping the great gobs of dirt and grease off it. Boy, is this going to be fun. It's another of those evenings when I come into the house and Lovely Linda says something like, "You look like a three-day old train wreck. Are you okay? Any major damage?"

And I reply, "Darlin', I couldn't be better. You probably don't want to hear the details . . . "

"I don't."

"But I'm on top of the world. Share a little cheap champagne with me? I'm going upstairs to take a shower and slip into something more comfortable."

"I think I'm going to get a headache."

Well, anyway, it's the thought that counts.

Day 49 hours	4.0
Total project hours	195.0

Shot Tires and the World's Cleanest Parts Tractor

<table>
<tr><td>WELSCH
WEATHER
REPORT</td></tr>
<tr><td>Bitter cold.</td></tr>
</table>

WINTER IS HERE AGAIN, AND POOR ol' Woodpecker still sits on her blocks, her second winter in the shop. What's more, there are new problems. The front tires I thought were good, aren't. I mount them on the new hubs and lower the tractor from the jacks. Air blows audibly from holes in the rock-hard rubber. Nothing to do but buy tires, have them mounted on the wheels, and try again. Not much to be done until that process is taken care of.

I take the time again to do things right, even though my natural inclination is to get the job finished—just *finished*—no matter what. Using chases, I clean out the threads of the lug holes in the wheels and the lug bolts. They're a mess. It's a good thing I did it right. I'd have had trouble again down the line if I hadn't.

On the rear I still have the iron wheels with lugs, pretty much just to get her out of the shop when the time comes to pull-start her. Or maybe I should be more humble—*try* to pull-start her. A few weeks ago I pulled a wreck into my dismantling bay outside and started taking it apart before the weather got too bad. About all that remains now is getting the engine out from between the frame side bars and getting the back wheels off. That's the good part. This wreck, for what little good metal is on it, has two passable back tires. I'm hoping they will be the ones that will wind up on The Woodpecker and save me financing that problem. I can't afford to buy new rear rubber for these toys.

In the meanwhile, I spend time in the second bay of my shop, working on what I hope will be a test stand engine. I am once again surprised by what I find. Remember when I said that all the books say that when you find a block that has structural cracks—not just water jacket sides punched out from frozen coolant but *broken* block members, between or around the cylinders, you might just as well throw it away? Well, this is maybe the 20th Allis Chalmers WC block I have now looked inside of . . . and all but one has been cracked between cylinders. This one is too.

This time, when I take the oil pan off my test engine, I find the rod cap nuts don't have cotter keys through a castellated nut, just castellated nuts, sitting there, on those oil-soaked rod bottoms that slam and vibrate at a horrendous rate when the engine runs. Is that possible? What keeps them on there? Isn't that dangerous? I don't know. Don't ask me. This is the best engine I've ever dismantled and it doesn't have cotter keys holding the rod cap nuts. Go figure.

Moreover, this is an engine I pulled off a total wreck, one of the most disreputable tractors ever hauled into this yard and dumped near the shop to be dismantled for parts. Yet at every turn, I have been surprised at the great shape the engine is in. I have never opened one in better condition. The sleeves are clean and bright, the bearings are relatively tight, nothing is broken (other than the block!), everything is clean, comes out smoothly, cleans up pretty.

So, what do you suppose the story is? Why was this machine discarded while it was in such good shape? Why is this engine so sharp but was housed on a frame that was a rusty, useless mess? Those are mysteries that will never be solved, I suppose.

While I'm waiting for the new tires and the front end, and a new bushing for the governor control rod on the test engine, I work on the pile of mail on my desk. Gladys Bleyl, a fellow columnist in The Nebraska Farmer magazine, writes that she likes my book *Old Tractors and the Men Who Love Them* in part because it reminds her of an uncle. Now get this: at the end of World War II, he needed a tractor, but of course none were available . . . so he made one. He just *made* one. Whew. Is that self-reliance, or what?!

Me, I can't even figure out what to do with all the problems that confront me with this machine someone else built. The Woodpecker has an unusual magneto—at least unusual in terms of what I'm used to on these machines. It's a Fairbanks-Morse 4-B. I've never figured out how to set the magnetos on the other WCs I have, even though I have a tech sheet on them. I can read the directions, but I can't understand them, no matter how hard I try. I'm an educated man, but just not educated in this particular direction. So where do I start?

Somewhere I notice that Warren Jensen of Jensales Company, an antique tractor information publisher, has a variety of tech sheets available on old tractors. I think I saw it in an advertisement in an antique tractor magazine I subscribe to, maybe *Antique Power* or the *Old Allis News*. So, I dig around. But I find that in addition to individual tech sheets at a pretty reasonable price—a few bucks a pop—Jensen has a huge compendium of every damned old magneto he could find information on, 500 pages of details.

Now, do I spend a couple bucks on exactly what I need at the moment, or go ahead and invest in the big volume on the theory I'll be working on old tractors for a long time, and even though they're all one model, they probably have different mags on them now and again? You know the answer: Do it right the first time. I call for the big volume. It is an encyclopedia of information and I'll never have to worry about magneto specifications again. Think of the price that thing will bring when Linda has the big auction sale after I go to Tractor Heaven. I'm betting her new boyfriend will put his arm around her shoulder and say, "Linda, that Rog must have been quite a guy." (Curiously, totally without warning or explanation, a fan blade will break off one of ol' Rog's WCs someone was trying to start and imbed itself right in his . . . well, never mind. It's just a fantasy.)

Not much of a day on The Woodpecker, but a good day in the shop. Won't be long now, I tell myself: Once I get the tires on, the only thing left is the magneto, although that is a mighty big "only." Then, some nice day after the worst of winter is over, we'll haul her out and give her a try. We're now at 14 months on this project. I wish I could get things moving more quickly. [Author's Note: Oh man, does this guy have some surprises in store for him!]

Day 50 hours	2.0
Total project hours	197.0

The Wonders of Electronics

I may never understand magnetos, generators, and distributors. God knows, I've tried. Nonetheless I am always looking for little clues and hints that might help me along. A long letter from Dave Walleck of Lincoln, Nebraska, recounts an experience that is painfully close to many of my own. Since it is probably also close to many of yours, I include Dave's letter here for your profit and enjoyment too.

Dear Roger,

I remember the time when we hooked up the 1929 Whippet [automobile] by a chain to a tractor (an Allis) to start it for the first time. It was a six-cylinder. We pulled it and it would fire, but cough and sputter and backfire more often. So we stopped and carefully set the timing again. Same thing. Repeated. Same thing. You know how that goes. When we were about to declare that it would never run again we decided to set the distributor timing one more time. In the process, when we were hand-cranking the engine ever so slowly to set the timing, it hit us. We had worked on numerous Chevys over the years but the Whippet had a distributor rotor that rotated in the opposite direction! So that six cylinder was trying to run on only two! We changed the spark plug wires on four of the holes, pulled the car a short distance, and listened to it run for the first time. Sounds like an experience you might have had.

—Dave Walleck

It is an experience I've had. And boy, is Dave ever right.

Houston, We Have Ignition (Sort of . . .)

WELSCH WEATHER REPORT

A month or so later, but still bitter cold. We are in the middle of winter, after all.

I MEANT THIS JOURNAL TO SERVE as a guide to newcomers in tractor restoration so they'd have an idea of how things go, just a hint of how things work in reality. For the past month I've dinked around in the shop now and then, not getting much done, and working on my test-stand engine when I was out here. Nothing much seemed to be happening on The Woodpecker. I got some cheap front tires from Al up at the filling station in town. He had to do a lot of grinding on the old rusty wheels to make them hold a tire, but he did it. I got them on the tractor, even though I can now see how warped and bent up they are. Well, The Woodpecker will never pull a plow, or run very far at road speed, or toil in the field for hours in the summer sun, so they'll probably do. (Yes, I know I said that since we're doing things here we might as well do them right, but . . .)

So, I put the tires on the wheel and the wheels on the tractor. I check fluids in the rear end and rear drives. I dismantle and clean up the magneto. I blow out fuel lines and check the carburetor. I pour oil over the rocker arms so it runs down over the lifters and cams before dropping to the oil pan . . . and suddenly there is oil everywhere. The plugs are tight. The gasket is holding. So . . . ? On the back of the pan, right in a flat spot, near no creases, no apparent damage or even a scratch, oil drips generously out of a pinhole. I try cleaning the wound and applying Weld stuff . . . it still leaks. How could there possibly be a hole in the pan that I didn't see when I was cleaning it up? I scoured that thing. Eventually I'll drop the pan and repair the leak from the inside, but for the moment I slip a small rubber O-ring over a sheet metal screw and screw it into the hole.

On one warm, balmy morning, I pour some water into the radiator . . . and now there is water everywhere, making nice little rainbows all over the shop floor. The gaskets are okay, the water manifold is okay . . . the water is coming from the bottom, most remote, most difficult to reach hose connection. Apparently, when I put the radiator on, somehow I missed tightening this one hose clamp. Now I have to struggle and bust my knuckles to get the job done.

I tend to such little jobs and disasters now and then, 15 minutes at a time, over the period of a month. I don't get a straight hour ever. Well, that's not quite true. I have the time but I'm getting tired of this project. It seems so far from success. There are so many enormous failures, so few small successes at this point. How curious that there were all those times I thought I was near success!

Now I am down to the hardest part—the magneto. I can no longer avoid the snag. I know absolutely nothing about electricity or magnetos, Jensales guide or not. I know I need help at this point, but hate to ask it of my friends, who have their own jobs and projects after all.

I look at the tractor, nearly ready to try out, and wonder. Late that same afternoon, three of my best, most mechanical buddies show up—Dennis (also known as Bondo), a farm boy and auto-body worker, Dan, a farm boy and plumber, and Melvin Nelson, a farm boy . . . and master mechanic, *specializing in electrical systems and magnetos*. I haul out a cold case of beer. We look at the tractor. We hover. We dance around it. The boys start to probe here, turn there, check this, look at that. They turn the crank and check valves. They approve of what I've done. Now they're caught up in the challenge. "Put her at top dead center," someone says, and fully willing to take advantage of this gift from the gods of internal combustion, I dive under the tractor and turn the fly wheel until the big F for "fire" appears in the middle of the inspection port.

The Boys confer, argue, drink more beer, talk, look, adjust, and try out. Then someone says, "Let's roll 'er out and see what happens." EEEEEK! For the first time in 16 months The Woodpecker rolls out of the shop into the light of day. I run to get my farm tractor, the International 300, and someone finds a tow chain. With far too little ceremony, Bondo, the auto-body repairman jumps onto the 300 and directs me to the seat of The Woodpecker, and we go down the lane. Someone yells and I pop the clutch. Nothing. Well, not for a few yards. Then there is a puff of smoke from the exhaust stack. A few bangs, a few firings. I'm encouraged. Melvin signals a stop.

The Boys hunker over the engine while I sit on The Woodpecker, hopeful. Bondo jumps back into the seat, and we give it another try. More bangs, more firings, four, five, 10 firings in a row. Dan runs alongside the tractor making adjustments, stumbling along a couple feet ahead of the gouging steel-lugged wheels. An OSHA official witnessing this debacle would have a conniption.

We are so close. Sometimes the engine runs independently for several seconds, but . . . it is still not really running. Finally, Melvin takes apart the magneto again and finds that the linkage with the governor is worn and loose. Any sort of accurate adjustment seems impossible. Do I have another mag? Yes, as a matter of fact I do. I run to get it. Melvin puts it on. This time the tractor fires enthusiastically, nearly running with a sustained roar. Oil and water spew. Melvin adjusts. We try again, and again, and again, and again.

Lovely Linda and I were supposed to go out to supper tonight, but now the sun is going down and I am filthy. But lovely friend that Linda is, she realizes how important this curious, dirty, loud, violent ritual is for me (and my friends). She brings us some hot chicken gizzards and gets out of the way. We try again and again and again and again. Once the engine runs hard and long before dying. We discover the fuel line is hopelessly clogged. If it hadn't been, we might have had the problem whipped. But it was. So we haul The Woodpecker back to the front of the shop and use the electric winch to haul it back in.

She's back in the shop, back where she's been sitting for a year and a half now, but she did run. The Woodpecker did run.

Up at the town tavern, eating burgers, we feel a little let down that we couldn't really tell everyone The Woodpecker ran in the full sense of the word. They do ask. Filthy, smelly, oily, exhausted, we become the focus of the small-town tavern that evening. Everyone has been following my progress, and set-backs, with this machine for almost two years now.

Becky, Bondo's wife, comes in and sits with us. All the while we'd been working on The Woodpecker, Bondo's little five-year-old son Ben has been with us, mostly sitting on Bondo's lap as he drove the 300 towing the old Allis and, awestruck, watching us men at our mysterious, loud, violent tasks. "And what did you do all afternoon?" Becky asks her little boy.

He sweeps away our disappointment when in perfect imitation of the serious faces he had been watching all afternoon, he bangs his little fist on the table and says, "Darn tractor . . . won't run. Darn tractor . . . won't run. Darn tractor . . . won't run. Darn tractor . . . won't run." Well, that pretty well sums up the days' activities, all right.

The next day I have to go on a business trip, but before I leave, I go to the shop to look over the damage. I picked up tools and parts scattered around the yard and along the road, left-over from our marathon mechanics session the evening before. I pat poor ol' Woodpecker and tell her things will be better, that I'll fix up the problems and repair what damage I can. In the hours of dragging her up and down the lane we pretty well destroyed our road (if you haven't seen what iron tractor lug-wheels can do to a road, it's not easily imagined) but what's worse, we shook loose anything on the tractor that wasn't snugged down to begin with. The reverse lock on the shift lever dangles at an angle. The shift lever itself wobbles at a goofy angle. Water drips from a hairline crack at a bottom fitting. Again, I pat The Woodpecker. "I'll try to cheer up if you will, old girl."

But that's not the end of this particular story. That afternoon I set off for Lincoln, 125 miles away. As I drive, I think about the tractor, promising myself and it that I will spend another day soon doing what I can to prepare it for another seminar with The Tractor Trio. I get about a 100 miles away from home when I see that I need to stop for gas, so I pull into a service station and step out of the car. I gasp in disbelief. It is so cold, the wind takes my breath away. Wow. The temperature must have dropped 50 degrees since I left the farm. Wow. It's a good thing we worked on The Woodpecker while the weather was half-way decent, I think.

Then it hits me like a brick in the middle of my forehead. The radiator and block are still full of water. I listen to the radio. It's now 20 degrees. It's supposed to be sub-zero by midnight. It won't rise above 10 degrees all of tomorrow. The shop is good shelter, and it does tend to preserve temperatures. But the temperature's not going to stay above freezing in the shop for the two days until I get back. I think about calling my buddies. Can't do that. Haven't the slightest notion where they are today. Can't have just anyone going into the shop with all those tools.

I pick up my cellular phone and call Linda. "I love you, darling, and it sure was super how you supported us when we were trying to get the tractor going last night. You're something special, love," I tell her.

"Okay, what do you want?" she responds.

Now, I don't know if Linda knows how to hold a wrench. I have seen her drive nails—with a shoe. I don't need the "No Gurls" sign hanging on my shop door because on those rare occasions when Linda does come out to tell me something or another, she says two things as a part of the ritual: 1) "Are you sure you have enough ventilation in here?" and 2) "You call this fun, right?"

I take a deep breath. "Yes, my beloved wife and best friend in this whole, wide world. Lovie, it's going to freeze hard tonight and if you don't go out and drain the engine and radiator on The Woodpecker, the block will crack and the radiator will bust up. All the work I've been doing for almost two years now will be lost."

"Tell me what to do."

I try to describe what a drain spigot looks like and where they are on the tractor. (If you think that's easy, give it a try for yourself.) I tell her where the pliers are and how to turn the spigots. "Let the water just drain on the floor. It doesn't matter," I tell her.

"I'll call you back," she says.

I drive on through the darkening gloom and cold, imagining that woman going out through the growing storm to that dank, stinking shop, locating the drains on that oily, dirty tractor, locating pliers, reaching down into all that cold, hard, greasy iron, turning the spigots, jumping back when the icy, rusty water spurts out onto the floor. I imagine some day reading this story in a woman's magazine special article, "Can This Marriage Be Saved?"

A few miles down the road, the telephone rings. I answer. "Done," she says. I think about joking and asking, "All three drains?" but I sense this is not the time for humor. One thing is clear: I owe this woman, and I owe her big. For all the noise I've made about women and how difficult they are, I spend a couple days drenched in humility. Who cares if they understand old tractors if they understand old men who love old tractors? One thing for sure, whatever this darling of mine wants for Valentine's Day, it's hers. I once had a Romeo pal who said that all women are the same once the lights go out. Not when the lights go out in the shop, old buddy, not when the lights go out in the shop.

I should probably note, because I'll bet you're wondering, what happened when I got home a couple days later and went out to the shop. I found she had done the job precisely right, and in the process had saved The Woodpecker. A couple cans of beer we had left sitting on the bench during our evening's work the week before froze solid.

Time spent this entire past month, including the long Woodpecker session, but not Linda's work on the drain spigots	5.0 eventful hours
Total project hours	202.0

Dan and Bondo's Tractor-Starting Machine

WELSCH WEATHER REPORT

It has been bitter cold for weeks—below zero.

I BUILD A FIRE IN THE STOVE, TURN on old-fashioned rock 'n' roll, and work at my bench, watching the snow and cold outside the window. I clean the gas line on The Woodpecker, since that was clearly a problem when we got her started a couple weeks ago. There's not much more I can do until the weather turns warm, and we can again drag her up and down the lane, trying to get her running.

Maybe. Today I'm sitting at my bench, cleaning rocker arms from the test-stand engine I've been working on, whistling, singing, generally enjoying life. At some point I turn around, probably feeling two pair of eyes on me, and there stand my friends Dan and Bondo, laughing at me. They stomp the snow off their boots, check what I'm working at, make sure I've cleaned out the fuel line, warm their hands at the fire . . . and start making measurements on the front of The Woodpecker.

Seems they've been doing some thinking. It just doesn't make sense, they tell me, informing me of something I already know, to drag these tractors around the farm trying to get them started. What I need is some kind of starter. They look over the belt drive pulley and make some calculations. They look at the PTO. Then they decide that what they will do is weld up a box to fit on the front end pedestal, using four of the eight front-end mounting bolts. They'll put a bearing in here and put an over-run clutch PTO shaft in here (so when the engine starts, the shaft is essentially disconnected). One end of the shaft will fit into the crank socket on the engine to be started, the other onto the PTO of another tractor. When I want to start an engine, I can just back up a running tractor to the shop door, connect the shaft to the engine to be tested, and pop the clutch. Then we can work on the timing, carb adjustments, magneto, oil pressure, whatever, *inside the shop*, without two people driving (one the

tow tractor, the other the engine in question) while others run along side with screwdrivers and pliers, inches ahead of those crushing steel lugs, with, as Bondo puts it, " . . . untied shoe laces dangling just inches in front of the iron."

Sure would be nice. Will they get it done? Hard to say, but it's a great idea. Since they're the ones who usually wind up in the gathering dusk, after a 12-pack of beer, in imminent danger of a horrible death under the steel wheels of one of my ancient tractors, they just might do it. My bet is they won't do a thing until I have another tractor just about ready to go and then, in an hour or so, they'll put together this magical device.

It doesn't hurt that the word has gone out from the town tavern than I have ordered the champagne for The Woodpecker's Recommissioning and Coming-Out Party, definitely the highlight of Dannebrog's (if not Nebraska's) social season. There are still weeks of work to be done, and I'll want to scrub her up a little for the occasion, and I have to get rubber on back wheels, and, perhaps most of all, the weather is going to have to do some fancy warming before I'm ready to head up an Allis Chalmers WC parade into town for the party. But the whiff of celebration is in the air.

(I haven't spent more than an hour on The Woodpecker since the last entry, and I don't think Dan and Bondo's plans for a starting device count, so the total is still 202.0 hours. Maybe a metric year is more like twice the length of the regular 365-dayer.)

An Unexpected Treasure

WELSCH WEATHER REPORT

A hot summer day . . . but then why not? It's June!

HEY, WAIT A MINUTE. WASN'T there snow on the ground the last time I wrote about being in the shop? So what happened? Where have I been all this time? I have been tied down with work . . . too tied down, too much work, not enough shop time, and that's for sure. As a direct result of that overwork, I had a heart attack a couple months ago, not long after Day 52, and there's nothing like a heart attack to slow up good tractor work! So, I have spent some time getting my priorities straight, dumping the work that stressed me most, losing a mess of weight, getting on a regular exercise schedule.

I ask the doctor (the one who understands, the one who does a little tractor restoration of his own) if my shop work, with all its inevitable emotional frustration and physical damage, contributed to my problems. Far from it, he assures me. In fact, it turns out that my cardiac problems are not the result of vein sludge but of stress and tension. Hence, I need *more* shop time! I am relieved, not only because I want more shop time but because for years I've been arguing that this would have happened to me a lot earlier if I hadn't had the time I did have in the shop. I simply don't want to believe that having that much fun, enjoying life that much, getting such pleasure is all as dangerous as the religious zealots and prudes would have us believe. I want to believe that such pleasure is just as much a gift of God as our trials and tribulations are somehow divine ordinance, too. Doc Lawton says that shop work is good for me, and I believe him. Tell your spouse that the next time he or she grumbles that you're spending too much time in the shop!

I had a few weeks of recovery, but slowly and surely, I've worked my way back out to the shop. I've done a little welding here and there—put together a neat coffee table made out of an old cookstove top and finished up some little things with The Woodpecker—putting the valve rocker cover back on, for example. Also, I got a letter the other day from folks I haven't heard from for, oh, maybe 12 years—Berniece and Don Jeffries. They're Mom and Dad of Sweet Allis, the very first Allis WC I ever got, some 20 years ago. This first Allis was given to me by a friend, who bought it originally as farm equipment from another farmer—Don Jeffries—who used it for decades in his own fields. I met them when I went to their farm to pick up a couple pieces of machinery, notably a pull-type, two-bottom plow. I cut one of the bottoms off and use it to dig furrows for tree planting.

Anyway, the Jeffries, it seems, are leaving their old farm and in cleaning up the sheds found a stock of parts they had accumulated when they were using Sweet Allis, and they wondered if I could use them. Of course I can use them!

So they drive out with a trailer-load of goodies—carbs, mags, air cleaners, a couple of uncracked blocks, a gear box, a brand spanking new camshaft still in the original Allis Chalmers box, three pristine hoods, 10 sleeves, 10 good pistons (and a couple of shot ones), bolts, nuts, brackets, that kind of thing. We unload all the parts, go to town for lunch at Harriett's, and then come to the unpleasant part of such events—business. There is a certain protocol to it all, a set of standard openers:

"Well, what are you going to need for all that stuff we just unloaded?"

"I sure don't know. What do you think it's worth to you?"

"Are you going to make me do both the buying and selling here, Don?"

"I know what all that stuff would cost out of a catalog . . . "

"Oh, I do too, Don. And I appreciate you delivering too."

"Do you suppose you could handle $100."

Now, anyone who knows his business knows that at this point I should have offered something like $50—akin to stealing, but I just don't have it in me. Especially when I took a second look at that pile of parts—already taken off the tractor, some of it new, most of it cleaned, all of it usable—a PTO shaft and two PTO gear boxes, two heads, a couple generators, a starter, three clutches, three oil pumps. Frankly, this is a treasure-trove for me. A problem for Don, a bunch of dirty, oily, rusty junk to almost anyone else, a chest of rubies and diamonds for me. The delivery charges alone would be $100 if I ordered this stuff out of a catalog. If one of the carburetors is good, it's worth a 100 bucks, and the rest of the goodies are gravy. How could I argue with that?

"You have a deal," I say, and reach for my checkbook.

As the Jeffries pull out of the yard, Don rolls down the window of his pick-up truck and asks, "You wouldn't be interested in a WD, would you?"

"Well, uh, sure," I sputter, having never really thought about moving up to a WD. (For those of you who are not familiar with Allis Chalmers tractors, the WD was next in line after the WC, manufactured from 1948 to 1954—the WC was turned out from 1933 to 1948. WDs are slightly more sophisticated, with a "live" hydraulic system, a little body streamlining, a hand clutch, foot brakes, starter, generator, lights, fancy stuff like that!)

For a couple days after I wave the Jeffries out the lane, I haul stuff into my parts bay and tuck it away on my shelves. I tell myself I should call a couple friends who have Allises and tell them that I have parts if they come up short. Something about generosity and friendship makes you all the more generous and friendly. I guess that's why this whole thing about old tractors and the good folks (mostly good folks, anyway!) makes it such a wonderful way to spend time and energy.

So, a couple weeks later Don shows up in my yard with yet another Allis, this one a WD. I decide to do a little work on it—replace a gasket in the rocker arm cover, clean up the bottom side, tighten up a wobbly front end, which means I once again need to pull The Woodpecker out of the shop.

Now, here she sits, and I don't have any excuses not to get rubber back on her and get that loose magneto fixed, to get her running and have that party. Maybe even before I reach the dreaded point of being a full year past my original deadline.

What with the new gasket on the rocker arm cover and pulling her out of the shop, I suppose I've spent another hour with The Woodpecker. I know what it will be like getting those liquid-filled, monstrously heavy, incredibly clumsy back wheels on, however, so there are still a lot of tough hours to go. I keep telling Linda not to worry about my heart. This is the kind of thing that's good for it. She's not convinced. I am.

| Day 53 hours | 1.0 |
| Total project hours | 203.0 |

DAY 54

Wheel Therapy

**WELSCH
WEATHER
REPORT**

Another Nebraska summer is here in all its glory, but mornings and evenings are still cool enough to get some outdoor and shop work finished.

YESTERDAY EVENING AFTER SUPPER and the news programs, I ventured out into the heat to get a little exercise, since I've been trapped at my desk all day. I loosen all the lugs on the left wheel. I take off all but two, and I consider what lies ahead. If you haven't worked with tractor tires before, they are huge and heavy. On an Allis WC, they aren't anywhere close to the size of the giants on modern tractors—the listed size is 11.25 x 24, as high as my lower chest, wide as my extended reach. I am told by folks who know that when they are filled with the saline solution that gives them traction and stability, they each weigh 400-500 pounds. This is not an easy size and weight for a single person to handle, no matter how big and strong he or she is.

I've been feeling a little puny, let's remember. If one of these things tips a little too far in any direction, the only thing I'll be able to do is get out of the way, just as quickly as I possibly can. Then I'll have to pick it up with the front-end loader on my working tractor.

In the past I have used the stationary hoist in my dismantling bay, or my engine hoist, or the tractor loader to move tires around and get them close to the axles. None of these methods has proven very successful; I've gotten the job done, but definitely not easily. I'm not at all sure what my strategy will be this time, but since the tractor is sitting outside, near nothing I could use for a hoist or crane, I'm going to have to come up with something new.

I amble over to the dismantling deck where I took apart the last tractor and left the tires leaning against posts. I pull one of the wheels from the post and measure its heft. It is heavy, of course, and clumsy, and slosh-es menacingly. I give a test roll. It moves fairly easily away from the post across the grassy but level ground in front of my shop. I lean the wheel ever so slightly toward me because that gives me more control than if I were trying to hold it up across the lean, but I also know that this puts me in a little more jeopardy should the thing start to fall.

I very carefully take a step and roll the wheel. It rolls easily. I take another step and roll. I move my hip into the back side of the tire and swivel it into a slightly better angle toward the tractor. Another step, another, another. It becomes very clear that if I am careful and deliberate in this operation, it will go. I am near a cedar tree so I maneuver the tire and wheel to the tree and lean it carefully against the trunk—not so steep that it is likely to fall over on the ground during the night, not so shallow that I won't be able to raise it to the vertical again tomorrow.

I return to the house a little more optimistic than before.

| Day 54 hours | 0.5 |
| Total project hours | 203.5 |

Left Wheel, No Problems

I START ON THE TIRE AND WHEELS right away in the morning. I jack up the left rear end of the axle and block it solidly with large, square wood blocks and 2x8 scraps. I remove the final two lugs and pull the steel-lugged wheel from the tractor without problem. I remove all the lugs from the hub—not just the nuts, but the lugs themselves, which I had previously taken out to clean. They come out easily.

I roll the steel wheel away and begin the process of moving the rubber-tired wheel into location. I am still afraid of this blasted thing, and I move another tractor so its right back wheel is within a yard of the axle end I am working on. I don't know enough about these things to know if I am doing the right thing or inviting disaster: If the tractor falls off the blocks, or the wheel tips and falls, is it likely to trap me against this other tractor tire and wheel, or will the tire and wheel keep the weights from falling on me? I look the situation over and conclude the latter.

I roll the tire and wheel into place without too much difficulty. The tractor's hub is about six inches too high for the rubber-tired wheel, and this is where things turn right for me. I crank up the jack and remove one of the big 8x8 blocks. I can tell by looking at the set-up that if I lower the jack, the hub will now be too low for the tire. I insert more 2x8s and 1x8s until the hub seems just about at the right height, maybe a touch high. I lower the jack. The tractor sinks onto the blocks. Close. I rock the wheel onto the hub, and even though the hub does indeed rest a half inch or so high for the wheel, at least the wheel is now started onto the hub. I raise the jack, remove another 2x8, and insert a 1x8. Lower again. Still a trifle high. I jack it up and remove the 1x8. Lower again. This time the hub is

almost exactly right. I pull the wheel back from the hub and turn the hub so the lug holes are close to the holes on the wheel, and I lean the wheel back onto the hub.

I feel uneasy sitting between the wheel I am installing and the one on the tractor I put in place to protect me but I see very quickly that I can insert one of the lugs and a nut almost without effort, which I do, and now the wheel is secured by at least one lug and nut on the tractor.

I work my way around the wheel inserting more lugs and loosely attaching nuts where I can. I have invented (I think) a neat device for situations like this. I call it a "blind" nut. I took a lug nut and welded one end shut. I did this by taking a washer that fits closely in the nut and then just welded it in place. I put this cul-de-sac nut on things like wheel lugs and then can use a regular box-end or socket wrench to screw in the lug. I do this with the lugs, attaching the lug nuts as I go. And then, there it is. The wheel and tire are on!! I jack the axle up, remove the blocks, and lower the wheel to the ground.

By now it is too hot to continue the process, but I decide to get a start so I can finish it off tomorrow. I loosen the lug nuts and lugs on the right-hand wheel, jack up the axle, block it, and remove all the lugs and nuts but two. Should be a cinch to finish the job tomorrow morning when it's cool again.

Day 55 hours	1.5
Total project hours	205.0

Breakin' Loose

Jerry Henneman of Woodinville, Washington, had a few nice things to say about *Old Tractors* and added a note about his experience with penetrating solvents, probably the single most consuming chemical concern of tractor restorers.

Dear Roger,

I've enclosed a page from last year's "Aircraft Spruce and Specialty" catalog. WD-40 has an extremely poor reputation among airplane mechanics, around here anyway. Seems to work okay initially, but not last long. Its use on airplanes is supposedly frowned on by the FAA, and prevailing rumor has it that it's mostly kerosene. LPS number one has very similar properties but is much longer lasting. I've seen it in hardware stores on occasion. It tends to be available at airport supply shops. LPS two is more the consistency of lubricating oil but it has better penetrating and moisture displacing qualities, and also seems to last longer. It's a lot like using regular lubricating oil except you have the perception that any moisture inside—perhaps a hinge—is going to go somewhere else. LPS three is more viscous and dries to a waxy film. I've mostly seen it used to protect bare metal parts of equipment stored outside. I have a layer under the liner of my pickup truck bed. And I keep the inside of the tailgate coated with it. Good stuff.

I've seen [Par-Al-Ketone] used mostly to lubricate and protect aircraft control cables, and as an anti-seize compound for nuts and bolts that are exposed to the elements. Again, good stuff.

The Aircraft Spruce and Specialty catalog is fun. It's intended for airplane builders and restorers and probably the best of its genre. Take a good look at a 1930s light plane sometime, something like an early Cub or Aeronca. The structural principles are a bit different from a tractor, but the functional simplicity is rather similar.

Also, if you haven't used the non-rebound hammer (also

known as a dead-blow hammer), try it the next time you're doing something like driving a drift. Instead of going "bang" and bouncing back from the blow, it'll go "thunk" and transfer most of the energy to whatever you're banging (or thunking) on. They're easier to control and less tiring to use.

I have indeed used a dead-blow hammer and I like them a lot for things like rapping on stuck pistons. I intend to send for an Aircraft Spruce and Specialty catalog the minute I finish typing this page! Sounds like fun and one of those obscure sources you'll never find without the help of a friend like Jerry. The address, in case you'd like to send for a catalog yourself, is P.O. Box 424, Fullerton CA 92632, phone 800-824-1930.

DAY 56

The Wheel Deal

AGAIN I SLOWLY WALK AND ROLL THE next wheel-tire combo into place. I decide not to use the protective tractor routine again, which turns out to be a good idea. I remove the last two nuts and lugs, dropping the steel-wheel from the hub . . . wait a minute. What's this? The wheel doesn't come off the hub. I tug at the wheel. Nothing. I pry with a long lever bar (made, I am told, from a Model T axle). Nothing. I look more closely. All I can figure out is that the wheel is hung up on a little lug that fits into what looks like a seventh lug hole in the wheel. I rock the wheel a little. Sure enough, the wheel is clearly jammed onto the little lug. I squirt some loose-juice on it (again, Kroil). I bang on it with a hammer. I pry. I wiggle. Nothing. I get a big sledge and really bang away. Nothing. I try to work a jack between the rear housing and reluctant wheel . . . won't fit. I get another jack and try the tractor frame and wheel . . . won't fit there either.

I am now sweating and fuming and falling further behind schedule. I should have known better than to think this was going to be easy. Finally I grasp both sides of the wheel firmly and pull and rock furiously at the same time . . . and I see the wheel slowly wiggling off the offending lug. More wiggle, more pull, and finally the wheel slides off the hub. Whew.

I roll the steel wheel to the side and walk and roll the replacement rubber into place. I use the same system of lining up the hub to the wheel, then the hub holes to the wheel holes, inserting one lug and nutting it to provide some security, and then blind nutting the lugs into the hub. There are a few adjustments and a little jiggling and wrestling, but no more than natural. (A phrase a friend of mine once used when I asked him if he had been cheating on his wife—revealing an attitude that probably was the reason she left him.) I tighten the lug nuts with a lug wrench, jack up the axle, remove the blocks, lower the tractor, and there The Woodpecker is, ready to be hauled off to Melvin Nelson's place so he can work on the magneto. I call him and tell him the situation, hoping he'll find time apart from the ferocious demands of farming to help me out with this machine. I also ask him if I couldn't come along and watch him when he works on the magneto. That way, I'll not only get a working tractor but a bit of an education. I'll take along a 12-pack of beer by way of tuition.

Day 56 hours	2.0
Total project hours	205.0

A-B-Cs of Engine Repair In the Field

I was astonished when I read through the next letter from Joe Shurtleff because I have had exactly the same experience! It's like the television set that won't work at home but is just dandy when you get it to the repair shop: sometimes a tractor won't run when you have it running but works just fine when it stops . . . sort of. As for having faith in a machine being pretty close to love, well, I once had a wife who amounted to a lot less than that, so faith strikes me as being pretty darn impressive!

Dear Roger,

I am a late 1916 model myself and, yes, I have just finished reading *Old Tractors and the Men Who Love Them*. I hesitate to use the word "love" in regard to tractors I've owned but there were those in which I had a lot of faith and I guess that's close. I have never owned a new tractor but I've ridden the unyielding seat of a Farmall regular on steel, whose angle tread was a farce and a fraud. A blacksmith—in Brock, Nebraska, I think—came up with the rail lug which was an improvement, only they wouldn't back up in mud. Spade lugs that bolted on wherever the holes would match supplied traction, but a steady pull on hard ground would shake your ancestors.

Wheels cut down and rubber mounted probably did as much toward the creation of future generations of farmers as any one thing. It convinced the diehard horse farmers that the wide distribution of weight packed the ground less than steel lugs.

I progressed from the old Regular to an F-20 Farmall. A little Allis C with a five-foot belly mount mower was my introduction to orange paint. Pound for pound it was the biggest and best tractor I ever owned, and it kindled my interest in ACs. I bought a WD, got an old square front WC for a back-up, then progressed to a WD-45, a D-17, and finally an early model D-19. I should have quit while I was ahead. My regard for the D-19 can be concisely put by saying I traded it for a rear-tine garden tiller and a paid receipt for the repair bill on the D-19.

The WD-45 epitomizes my faith in cold steel painted orange. It would start, it would run, and it would do its best to operate anything it was hooked to. The little C, however, kindled a feeling very close to affection. If you're still with me, I'll relate a tale you can tell at the tavern on an occasion when conversation slows to reruns.

The C-Allis and belly mounted mower was a handy piece of equipment, whether you were mowing weeds higher than the tractor, fence rows under barbed wire, or hay fields. This experience unfolded on a hot, dry afternoon in a 12-acre field of red clover. Third gear is not the recommended gear for mowing hay but with a sharp sickle, good guards, and dry conditions, it works. A spirit of adventure and no respect for your backbone helps. The red clover field was nearly square, and I hated to work square fields. With the belly mounted mower, slowing down for corners was chicken. You came to a corner, spun the steering wheel, hit the hand brake, and cut lovely square corners.

At mid-afternoon I was bounding along and the Allis lost power. I changed gears but I had a fuel problem. Water in the gas? I stopped, checked the sediment bowl, drained the carburetor, and went merrily on my way for about another round. Same thing. That routine continued through the following: Dumped the sediment bowl, took off the gas line at the carb and blew till the tank bubbled. (Which process leaves a lingering taste of gasoline in your mouth and a smarting sensation in your sunburn if you sunburn. I do.) The sediment bowl was originally fasted to the gas tank with two short nipples and a pipe coupling. Step by step, I proceeded from the carb to the gas tank. The gas would flow for a round or two and then wean. When I finally got to the pipe coupling, I found a very big and very dead bumblebee. There was enough resilience in his body to pack tight in the coupling as I bounced through the field, then it loosened up when I stopped for a moment.

Bumblebees seem to have a penchant for open holes when the wind blows across them. I figure it's the little unexpected things in life that filter in and around the planned things that make for a good solid life.

Take care—Joe Shurtleff

On the Road Again

I PIDDLE AROUND THE PLACE DURING the cool morning, retreat to my office when it gets a little warm . . . only to have buddies Dan and Bondo come in the door as I'm getting started on office work. They announce that they are headed over to Melvin's place—a good day to tinker, they announce, much as Lakota warriors used to shout that it was a good day to die. I take them out to my parts store to find the magnetos and a distributor they think they'll need to sort out The Woodpecker's problems, and they leave me to my work.

I peck away at my correspondence and work . . . all the while thinking of them having fun with my tractor. Finally I get the most crucial work done, tell Linda I'm diving out, and get to Melvin's farm yard just in time to watch The Boys try to start the tractor. (As it turns out, Melvin tells me, the magneto gear was one cog off in meshing with the timing gear; thing is, you have to remove the front cover of the magneto unit to see exactly what you are doing when putting the two halves together. It's not easy to do it right otherwise.) We throw a little gas in the tank and a chain around the front, roll out one of Melvin's big tractors and give The Woodpecker a tow. It starts. It not only starts, but starts easily. It not only starts easily, it runs well.

We make minor adjustments and watch things carefully, grinning like idiots. There isn't much conversation because The Woodpecker's roar prohibits all but the most basic sign language. Everything, as is usual in such processes, seems to leak. Coolant comes out not only from the hose fittings but from the head gasket. Oil spurts from the filter bracket, where I have a two-pint canning jar instead of a filter. Oil also comes

from the back of the oil pan—main seal or oil pan end gasket, we wonder? We drive the machine around the farm yard. It runs better and better at each pass. Heavy grease now runs from the rear axle—shot seals? We remain optimistic: just as it is not unusual to have such leaks, it is not unlikely that they will seal up again as seals soak and swell with hot oil, coolant, or grease.

The Boys stand in the door of Melvin's shop, drinking cold beer, listening to that ragged old engine roar, watching the tractor re-pave Melvin's driveway with spewings of oil. It just keeps running better and better. Then Bondo makes the mistake of taking a closer look. Ouch. The oil bubbling up in the fruit jar-cum-oil filter is taking on a creamy white color: Water is getting into the oil. A lot of water. Dan drives the machine back into the shop and we turn it off. Fluids continue to drip from every part of the machine.

We pull the rocker arm cover and retorque the head nuts . . . and they are loose enough to be a possible explanation for the problem with the water getting into the oil. Melvin drops a couple cooling system sealer tablets into the radiator. The rocker cover goes back on, and we start it again. It runs fine, and leaks considerably less. We decide that it runs so well, in fact, that we can just drive it the six miles back to my place from Melvin's, and so someone pours the remnants of his can of gas into the tank.

That's always a mistake—pouring remnants. I firmly believe that you should always leave a quart of gas in any can—maybe just discarding it.

There is water in that last cup or two of fuel, and gunk and crap and dirt and lumps.

Dan wins the lottery to drive Woodpecker and takes off down the gravel. We say our good-byes and thank-yous to Melvin, and start down the same road . . . only, a mile later, to find Dan standing in the road, dismantling the fuel system. The gas sediment bulb has filled with rust flecks and some sort of gunk from the bottom of Melvin's fuel can. So, we stand around another half hour, cleaning out jets, lines, carburetor, and filters, and re-assembling everything again.

Woodpecker starts right off again, however—a good sign—and this time Bondo starts down the long road toward my farm. Mile after mile this good ol' girl, once given up for junk, throbs along down the road. It is still throwing a little oil, grease, and water, and the ancient rear tires I mounted start coming apart, flicking bits of rubber back toward me, trailing behind in my pick-up truck. Then salt solution starts leaking from the tires, and the front tires wobble insanely. (The lug bolts seem firm enough, but it appears that the wheels are more badly bent than I thought.) As we pass through Dannebrog, the little town near my farm, the engine sputters. We are only a mile or so from my place, so we elect not to dismantle the carburetor again but to keep going, hoping we can make those last few hundred yards before the fuel is choked off entirely.

No such luck. Less than two hundred yards from my property line, she gives up and dies. So, again, we hook up a chain between my pick-up and the Woodpecker and drag the poor girl the last stretch. (When we park her near my shop for final work, we find . . . she's out of gas. She was willing, but we hadn't done our part.)

Tonight, after I shower off all the gasoline, oil, grease, sweat, and dirt, I make a new list:

- Find good front wheels
- Find usable tires for back
- Replace clutch portal lids
- Check back oil pan gasket
- Drain bad oil
- Replace with clean, dry oil
- Recheck oil pan gasket
- Wash dirt, oil, and grease off tractor

- Flush fuel system
- Start organizing for re-commissioning party
- Buy champagne
- Think about snacks
- Write invitation list
- Find good date to have the party
- Thank Melvin Nelson and pay him

You can't imagine how good it feels to write those last items. The end of a two-year project is at hand. The tractor is still a mess, anything but restored. It's not pretty, nor does it sound particularly good, except for those of us who have worked so hard to get it to this point. To us, it looks beautiful and its roar is music. The leaks and sputters mean little.

The tractor is still rusty, needs fenders and PTO platform, smells bad, misses an occasional firing. (Bondo listens to her for a moment and says, "Sounds terrific . . . for a John Deere. Why, Rog, those extra two cylinders are just spares, after all!") Maybe some day I'll get to that. But at this wonderful moment, that's not the point. The point is that two years earlier Jim Stromp was only saying the obvious when he said, "Rog, you got the Giltner running, and you got Roaring Orv running, but you'll never . . . NEVER . . . get this thing running!" I was only having fun and showing off when I accepted the challenge. It was only common sense to admit that this rusty wreck probably never would run again. But here she is, running. It doesn't matter what she looks like, or sounds like. She's running, and I did it.

Okay, WE did it. My friends and I. Friends here, from all over, some close friends, some friends I've never met. A stranger might look at The Woodpecker and, quite justifiably, see nothing but a piece of noisy junk, utterly worthless in the world of tractors, or for that matter in the scheme of anything that amounts to anything.

Not to me and my friends. To us, this thing is an icon, a symbol of everything that's good about life—friendship, work, fun, successes, failures and recoveries, salvage and salvation, ingenuity, respect—all in that noise, heat, stink, and ugliness.

You don't get it? Maybe it's just easier for those of us who think of ourselves as kin of each other and our old tractors, generators of noise, heat, stink, and ugliness. Maybe you have to be as old as one of these old tractors to understand what they mean. I don't know. I don't care. I know what the machine means to me . . . in a philosophical sort of way. Its message is not much more to me than good feelings, from beginning to end.

What about all those times recorded in this journal when I was angry, frustrated, injured, or confused? They don't matter now. Now I just see the ol' Woodpecker rolling down the road on her own power, a tractor that would never run again, running again. That's enough for me. The only time I've had a feeling like it is when I watched my kids graduate from high school and college. What about all the tough times leading up to that moment? They don't carry much weight when the flush of success fills the sky.

Day 57 hours	3.0
Total project hours	210.0

DAY 58

It's My Party

WELSCH WEATHER REPORT

A splendid autumn day.

ACTUALLY, FOR THE FIRST TIME IN these two years, I've been spending a good deal of time on the Woodpecker project in my office—making lists of everyone who's helped me over the years with The Woodpecker, putting together an order for champagne and food, printing and sending off invitations to the champagne reception for recommissioning The Woodpecker. The invitation is shown on the right.

The guest list so far looks like this:

PHIL HINRICHS: our postmaster, and an old Allis C man, but invited largely because he has handled so many packages of tools and parts over the years.

JIM COSSAART: an old windmill repairman, now a dental student, a man who has located old tractors for me, and a friend.

JEFF GRAVERT: a professional tractor restorer from Central City, the next town over, a friend and thoroughly good guy.

ROBERT AND CAROL PANOWICZ: Allis restorers from Grand Island—not far away—and the subject not long ago of one of my "Postcards from Nebraska" on CBSs *Sunday Morning*.

HILDER FAMILY: the Deutz-Allis dealers from Central City, old Allis people who really go out of their way to help old tinkerers like me.

JERRY AND CLAUDIA OBERMILLER: farmers, friends, implement dealers, and salvage buyers, who have helped me many a time in the past.

MELVIN NELSON: an incredibly talented mechanic and good-spirited gent, who is largely responsible for getting The Woodpecker "on her feet".

THIS IS TO INVITE YOU TO A

Champagne and Beer Reception

for

1937 Allis Chalmers WC

(Serial Number 56,999)
A Gift From James Stromp, August, 1994
To Be Re-Commissioned as

"The Woodpecker"

Said Reception To Honor Participants and Contributors
To The Woodpecker's Rebuilding

★★★★★★★★★★★★★★★★★★★★★★★★★

October 5, 1994, Saturday, 5-6 P.M. (at Precisely 6 P.M. You're
On Your Own)
* At Eric's Big Table Tavern *
Dannebrog, Nebraska

★★★★★★★★★★★★★★★★★★★★★★★★★

By Invitation Only; Regrets Only.

Expressions Of Sympathy To Lovely Linda;

Memorials To Dupah Tractor Rest Haven.

Bring A Spouse Or Love Interest (**But Not Both!!**)

Please note that Jim Stromp did present this tractor to me at our last re-commissioning (for "Roaring Orv") precisely one metric year ago with the clear intent of embarrassing me, sure as he was that this utter wreck of a tractor would never run again, and I swore that we would meet again at Eric's precisely one metric year later (26 King James months) to listen to her hum. His witness is that the tractor sat rusting in a wood lot for a good 35 years. It was one of the worst wrecks ever dragged into this yard, and that's a lot of wrecks. On that occasion I swore to prove Stromp wrong. That tractor now runs. This machine is anything but restored—it is battered, bloodied, noisy, rusty, leaky, even pathetic if you forget that it was delivered as a total wreck—but it runs. Be sure to be here to watch Strompy writhe in humiliation!! Even if you don't care about Jim Stromp, or tractors, come and pat ol' Woodpecker's battered body and be reassured that there may even be hope for you.

DAVE MOWITZ: editor at *Successful Farming*, the man behind that magazine's Ageless Iron series and the huge antique tractor shows in Ankeny, Iowa; he's an inveterate old-iron man.

STAN KOPERSKI: salvage dealer, who has quietly and kindly helped me find machines for the past four years.

KENNY PORATH: professional mechanic and neighbor, who has always been ready to help me through the tough places.

DON HOCHSTETLER: machinist and all-round handyman in town who is the real professor when it comes to old Allises—I've seen him repair a stuck transmission with the tools in his pocket!

MEL GRIM: retired proprietor of our town's service station and the man who gave me my first hints about mechanicking.

MEL HALSEY: mechanic and friend who has helped me with engine work and, most importantly, hauled tractors for me with his pick-up and trailer.

GAYLORD MICKELSEN: mostly just a good friend, but as I wrote on his invitation, his wife Judy is such fun when she has a glass of champagne that I just couldn't see my way through to not inviting *him*.

DENNIS "BONDO" ADAMS: auto body man and farmer, but also a tractor hauler, mechanic, and good ol' farm boy who has given me some of my best advice about tractors—and if he doesn't know the answer, always has a funny line about it.

DAN SELDEN: a plumber, but another of those farm boys around here who always seems to know a little something about everything—which is really handy when it comes to tractor restoration.

MICK MAUN: a mason and outdoorsman, but given a chance to bang away on an old tractor, can be counted on for a day's worth of hard, enlightened work and plenty of laughs.

STEVE AND LISA LINNEMEIER: in-laws, but Steve is the carpenter who built my shop so I'm inviting him anyway.

LEE KLANCHER: editor at Motorbooks who got me started writing about this wacky obsession.

SCOTT LEISINGER: our UPS man, and special honored guest at this occasion, since he has personally delivered into this yard 17 metric tons of tools and parts over the past two years—at least that's what Linda says.

AL AND LAVON SCHMITT: proprietors of the service station that was Mel's, all-round good folks, and Al is an absolute master mechanic, still at a loss about what to think about me and my working for fun at what he does for a living.

JIM STROMP: salvage yard owner with a gold mine's worth of Allis parts, and the man who threw down the gauntlet that brought about this book and its result.

DALE DUNCAN: something of a town character, a devoted Allis man, a source of information and encouragement throughout the Woodpecker project.

STEVE LEHN: Don Hochstetler's right-hand man, becoming something of a mechanic himself.

VERNE HOLOUBEK: another Allis man, originally a Nebraskan but now in Wisconsin, a man who understands the soul of farm and tractor work.

BART HULTINE: an Allis man, a good-spirited adventurer and generous friend.

DOUG RUBEN: a bright and interesting guy who almost got me that Porsche tractor I lusted for in my last tractor book.

GLENN KLUTHE: welder, source of the scrap iron with which I tried to learn a little about his art myself.

But guest lists and invitations don't count as real work on The Woodpecker. There is still a good deal of that to be done before the party—perhaps too much. I know I should have waited before sending out the invitations but, Jeez, I have to get this thing done before the snow starts to fly, or it'll be next summer—another year.

So, I go back to fussing with The Woodpecker, trying to deal with all the problems that showed up while Bondo, Dan, and I were driving her back from Melvin Nelson's place. I call Vern at T. O. Haas's tire place in St. Paul, our county seat, about my tire problems. Vern has always been helpful when it comes to tractor problems. (In fact, I should send him an invitation to the party too.) He does some digging and finds that center pivot irrigation units use the same size tire my Allis WCs do. They aren't authentic, but then I'm not in the business of restoration, certainly not at this point in this project; they are shallow-treaded and fairly light-duty, but then this tractor will never have to haul much more than me the rest of its life, and I've lost 60 pounds since last April. He comes up with good, suitable rubber at $260 a pair, which may sound like a lot for light-duty, non-authentic tires—but only if you've never bought tractor tires before. What I will do is use these tires as I use the lugless iron wheels I use on tractors I bring into the shop—as temporary service rubber just to get me there and back.

With all this in mind, I go to The Woodpecker to pull off the ruined tires—and find that whatever condition I thought the wheels were in, they are in fact rusted junk. I can't put even the irrigation tires on these things, especially since I intend to use these sets on a number of other tractors in years to come. I go to my tire pile and find four different wheels that are in better shape, load them into my pick-up truck with my front end loader, and take them to St. Paul to be tired.

Next I address the front wheels. I put new tires on the front a long time ago in this project, but as Bondo was driving back from Melvin's, me in tow, I could see that one front tire was almost wrenching the steering wheel from Bondo's hands, leaving a snake-like weave in the gravel road. The wheel is hopeless warped.

I jack up the front of the tractor, check the bearings to be sure the wobble isn't in them (it isn't—I re-did them during the shop work, I recall), and spin the wheel. As I look at it dead on, I can see a very pronounced wobble. I line up the side bead of the tire with the shadow the sun casts off the tractor frame and turn the wheel. It is very clear precisely where the distortion is in the wheel.

I remove the wheel. When it falls on the ground, back up, I can see quite clearly where the rim is twisted. Who knows? Maybe something hit the tractor when it was parked in the wood lot all those years, or Stromp or I may have bent it while hauling this poor orange wreck from one place to another. I consider the problem: what I'll probably need to do is take this wheel off, maybe even the other so the two front wheels will match, find two more (five lug-holers, not six lug-holers, which makes the task a little more complicated than it may seem), take them up to Al Schmitt, and have him switch tires. This means he may have to do major clean up and repair on the replacement wheels, since none of these things is ever in really good condition, no matter how good a condition they are in. (At this point in the book, you should be able to see the logic in a goofy statement like that.)

I sit and stare and think. And I remember. I was once tooling along down a mountain road somewhere in Colorado. My old friend Dave Ratliff, the very one who gave me Sweet Allis, my first old tractor, was with me. As I rounded a bend, suddenly right there in front of me, was a huge chuck-hole. I had three choices:

1) Swerve left and head-on into an approaching semi-truck and death.

2) Swerve right and over the edge of a hundred-foot cliff to certain death.

3) Hit the chuck-hole.

I hit the chuck-hole.

The consequences were instant and obvious: the tire was blown and the wheel hopelessly distorted. When I got the car safely stopped and off the road, we found our impression to be accurate. We replaced the ruined tire and wheel with one of those pieces of junk they now call a spare, knowing that if the damned thing would be good for only 30 or 40 miles on decent roads, on this mountain route, we'd be in trouble if we didn't get a real tire and wheel on the car at once.

We stopped at the first service station we came to, and from the way they greeted us, I wondered if they hadn't built that chuck-hole to their personal taste. "I think we cun let ya have a tahr for a hunnerd fiffy and a new whil for another hunnerd," the surly jerk in the tire bay of the service station announced.

I couldn't see an alternative so I was ready to cough up what amounted to extortion, but Ratliff didn't take the news well. "We'll give you a $75 for the tire," he said menacingly, which he could do very well.

"Well, okay," the grease-monkey said, obviously intimidated.

Ratliff picked up the twisted wheel and looked it over. "Give me that sledge," he said to the tire-boy. The tire-boy complied. Ratliff proceeded to put that wheel on the floor and pound the living hell out of it.

Now, I always thought wheels and tires were just another precision thing on a car. They need to be tooled and trimmed, balanced and honed to a degree of accuracy or they won't work. Dave taught me otherwise,

and probably the tire-boy too. He beat that wheel until it seemed straight to him, and he handed it to the tire-boy. "Mount the tire on that," he said, and the tire-boy did. I drove on that wheel for four or five years until I sold the car.

So, I re-consider the front wheel from The Woodpecker. I take a hand sledge, whisper a prayer to whatever gods Ratliff prays to, or pray to Ratliff, and I proceed to pound. Pretty soon the wheel looks straight-ish. I spin it on the sledge handle. It rolls fairly straight. I put it on the front hub with a couple bolts. I spin it. It still rolls straight. I tighten it up. It looks good.

At that very moment Bondo drives up. He looks at the wheel, spins it, and says, "See how pretty it is when you do the job right and put on decent wheels?" I tell him the story about Ratliff and the tire-boy. He shakes his head, pretty much like I did when it happened in the first place, and I'll bet the next time Bondo bends a rim, he'll fix the problem with a sledge hammer too. So goes the path of knowledge.

I locate, clean, and put on the clutch ports—and twist off a bolt in the clutch housing. My god, after all this work, all this time, all those broken bolts, I thought I was finished. As if the damned thing were made of cool butter, a bolt twists off with what seemed like no pressure at all. There is almost no chance that in the few days and little time I have left that I'll be able to get it out and replaced before the recommissioning party. I'll bet someone at the party—maybe several someones—will note the shiny end of that sheared bolt. I'll just have to laugh and tell the story.

I fill the crankcase with kerosene, figuring I'll rinse out whatever water remains from the previous oil and check for the source of the leaks. The first thing I see is a substantial leak, not at the pan gasket or rear seal, where we detected one earlier, but from near the oil filter bracket. I tighten the cover on the lifter case. The leak persists. I tighten down the filter bracket. Still leaks. I look closely . . . and I think I spot the problem: The filter has not seated solidly against the bracket. In fact, it appears that it won't seat solidly. I can't tell what the problem is but decide to do an end run and just put on a different filter. It seems to seat better, but there is still a bit of kerosene coming from the bracket. I may have to remove it and re-gasket it . . . or put up with the comments of everyone at the party to the effect of—"Got an oil leak at your filter bracket, you know."

Yeah, I know.

I continue the fill. Finally, when the level of the kerosene reaches the crucial level, it begins to drip heavily from the rear of the engine. Now, what I don't understand is, I thought I took care of this all when I had the engine on the stand in the shop. I thought I wouldn't have to crawl around under here with oil dripping in my hair and eyes . . . but here I am. I take off the oil pan and drag it into the shop yet once again. Now I'll have to scrape off all the old gasket and gasket sealer, crawl under the tractor and clean everything off under there, and try again, except with more difficulty since I'll be lying on my back under the machine. Damn and double damn.

What if the problem is the rear seal on the crankshaft? I don't know. I just don't know.

I watch the weather forecast and learn we're entering a rainy period just in these three weeks before the party, and I am going to be gone anyway all but a couple days during that time. What I therefore plan to do is haul out the sickle-bar mower I have been working on in the shop, roll The Woodpecker back in, and spend some evenings trying to get it at least into driving condition before the party. Wish me luck. I'll need it.

Day 60 hours	3.0
Total project hours	213.0

A New Addition to the Shop

WELSCH WEATHER REPORT

A gorgeous fall day.

I HAVE HALF OF TODAY AND HALF of tomorrow to get started on the last stages of correcting the problems that showed up with Woodpecker on her long trip back from Melvin Nelson's. I tidy up the shop, picking up tools, jacks, buckets, boxes, everything that might be in the way. With my International 300, I move out the Allis Model 5 rear-mount sickle bar mower I've been working on in the shop the past few months. It's not finished, and I'd really hoped to leave it in here most of the winter as I work on it, but The Woodpecker is the priority right now, and I need to get it inside: I have only three or four spare days to work on it between now and the recommissioning party. I can't afford to skip those days if the weather is bad. The mower comes out relatively easily.

Then I pull the long cable from a floor mounted winch I put in the front of my shop, a kind gift from ol' buddy Dan the Plumber, and begin the process of pulling The Woodpecker back to her old slot in the shop. This used to be an agonizing job because I used a come-along hand winch. I sat there on the floor for an hour or so "rowing" away, slowly moving a tractor in a few feet, jumping up, re-setting the steering wheel, winching, jumping . . . Now, I use a piece of line or chain to set the steering wheel where I want it and press a button on the winch's hand control and slowly but surely, the tractor rolls into its appointed place. (Later the next day I make a point of telling Dan thank-you again for thinking of me when he salvaged this particular piece of hardware!)

I clean off the pan I took off earlier, using my secret solvent—oven cleaner. I love this stuff. If you try it, be sure you're wearing goggles and stout kitchen gloves because it's nasty stuff, but it does the job of removing.

I can't see clearly where the leak might have been—there's a slight wrinkle in the gasket about where the leak is, so . . . ? Dan drops by and we take off the rear crankshaft cap and things look good in there, so it doesn't seem likely that the culprit is in the seal. There are a couple places where the oil pan doesn't seem to seat firmly. Maybe that's it? Don't know. I clean off the bottom of the block with putty knife, scrub pad, and oven cleaner.

Today's work is complicated a bit by my new shop companion, Cindy. Taking Pete Rauch's advice to invite Cindy Crawford to share my shop space while she's looking for new digs (after the break-up with Richard Gere), I have to keep my eye on Cindy to make sure she doesn't make a break for the door and get run over out in the farmyard. Okay, she's not exactly Cindy Crawford. Actually, she's Cindy *Clawford*, a stray, stub-tailed kitten that has become my shop cat. (But, as Linda reminds me, that's as close as I'm ever going to get to Cindy Crawford moving in anyway, so. . . . I did, however, once share a dressing room with the real Cindy Crawford at a television station in Kansas City, another story I'll tell you sometime when you're buying the single-malt scotch.)

At any rate, Linda and Antonia were having breakfast in town at Harriett's Cafe when they spotted this miserable, flea-bitten (seriously) little gray cat, mewing piteously. They took some food out to her. In her enthusiasm for real food, she bit Linda. (As I recall, Gere said Cindy Crawford did pretty much the same thing.) Linda called the vet, who said that either he could observe the cat for 10 days, at $8 a day, chop off its head and do an analysis (Linda's scream at that particular suggestion could be heard all the way into town), or we could watch the cat for 10 days. Right. Linda and Antonia will watch the cat for 10 days and then I'll drop it off the bridge into the river, right? Oh, sure. So, I have a new shop cat.

Actually, I have lamented in the past that my dogs can't get to the shop from their yard, and the cats don't come in there, so even though I am not at all a cat fan, I'm glad to have Cindy around. She'll enjoy this winter when I fire up the stove and spend long days in here while the snow flies. She's now working on adjusting to my loud rock 'n' roll and the smells and smudges of the place. The fun part is how she jumps ten feet straight up when I drop large pieces of sheet metal.

The problem isn't that Cindy takes time or bothers me or is in the way; it's just that I have to pause every so often and admire her antics around the shop. Right now she's eating a grasshopper who made the mistake of hopping in. I am hoping this is a sign that I've got myself a mouser. Bet the real Cindy wouldn't do that!

Day 59 hours	4.0
Total project hours	217.0

Big Mistake

Dear Roger,

I received a very special Christmas gift from my son this year—a copy of *Old Tractors and the Men Who Love Them*. I was in the porcelain appointed "reading room" this morning reading "Roger's Rules for Collecting Old Iron (and Living With Your Spouse)." My wife, Betty, who had been pretending to be sound asleep only minutes earlier (at 5:30, yeah, right) heard me laughing through the thin pine door so when I came back to bed she asked me what was so funny.

Do you see a fatal mistake in the works here? I could have said, "Oh, dear, it was that hilarious article in last month's *Smithsonian* Magazine about Vermeer's paintings," or any number of witty replies. But that is part of the problem. My witty replies usually occur to me a couple hours later and this time was no exception. So, instead, I said, eagerly shoving the book her way, "You've got to read this part here about rules."

Dumb, dumb, dumb!!! As I sat there re-reading over her shoulder and chuckling all over again, the light bulb slowly started to glow. Here I haven't even acquired my first rebuilder tractor yet and I've already spilled the beans. What could I have been thinking? (Or not!) Oh sure, I've got a 23-year-old John Deere but with a yearly oil change, a few tubes of grease, and 10 gallons of gas when the gauge needle gets into the red, it's a no-brainer.

In my short time in the "reading room" my plan had already begun to take shape. Okay, so I have a pretty good sized barn, but it's full of hay, and a 16-foot by 20-foot shed that my cousin and I built a few years back but it would never do. It already has a table saw, drill press, cutting torches, a few hundred board feet of treated oak lumber (wonderful stuff) and other essential odds and ends that take up too much space to leave room for working on a tractor. I actually fantasized about a three . . . no, make that a four stall shed with a wood burning stove, electricity, a concrete floor, etc., all for the sake of old tractors. I saw green instead of orange filling those stalls but what the heck.

Anyway, as my wife continued to read, I watched the corner of her mouth twitch occasionally but the full-blown guffaws I expected never materialized. When she finished reading, she just backhanded me in the chest and got up to get a cup of coffee. When she came back, she announced that we were going to Penney's in Springfield today to look at drapes for the living room.

In Rule Number Four you carefully placed a WARNING about buying your wife a tractor. Would it have killed you to put one of those warnings at the very beginning so guys like me whose gray matter may not rank up there with the likes of Albert Einstein or even Alfred E. Neuman on occasion, might stand a fair chance against their cunning and sometimes vindictive counterparts? So, now maybe you are starting to feel slightly guilty for your oversight. Well, good! Something as simple as, "Don't even think about letting your wife read this!" at the beginning would have given me all the pause I needed. I might even have gotten away with bringing home a 60-year-old rebuilder and passing it off as a parts tractor for my current whipper-snapper of a tractor, but hell no, not now.

In the future, please try to be more careful. Whenever I look at the new living room drapes that are most certainly in my future, I will be thinking of some poor old "B" shivering and rusting away in some fence row with a blackjack oak growing around the drawbar and blaming your sheer thoughtlessness for not warning me. Thanks a lot.

Anyway, I've sure got my work cut out for me. I may have to go all the way back to a steam engine and try to convince her that I'm bringing home an old wood-burning stove for the shed. At least that wasn't in your rules. If I'm not real *careful*, we may end up with carpet.

Your friend—Pete Rauch

Ouch, Pete. Frankly, I think you're not much of a man if you crawl around on your belly like that. Stand up for your rights, man. Show some backbone. Are you a man or a mouse? Who the hell is in charge there at the Rauch homestead?

Besides, I couldn't put a warning in the book because, well, er, uh, Linda wouldn't let me.

Next came a note from Pete Rauch to effect that Richard Gere had sold his Malibu home, bumping Cindy Crawford into the real estate market since she had no abode to fall back on, as it were:

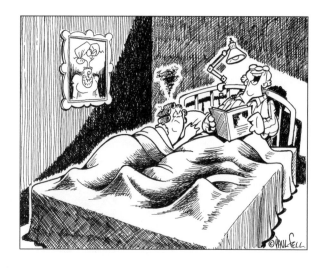

Dear Roger,

I saw this little dab of news in the Springfield paper and thought I would pass it along as a potential golden opportunity. I was thinking that now that Cindy's homeless it might be your big chance to bring on a "helper" for your shop. If she could keep all that hair under a DeKalb cap, you could get her a couple or three sets of loose coveralls, cover her little mole with a dab of grease, and pass her off to Linda as Cousin Spud from Eagle Rock, Missouri. (Son of your black sheep Uncle Dub that your Mom never talks about so please Linda, don't mention it to her because she would only be embarrassed and we don't want to get anything started . . . get the idea?) Your newly acquired shop helper would, of course, not want to be a bother so (s)he would be staying out in the shop. That corner that's being used for piling parts and junk could be cleaned out and a cot brought in. I can see great possibilities as long as winter is here. When spring gets here and the coveralls get to be too uncomfortable, you're on your own. If this works out, you owe me, pal.

—Pete Rauch

P.S. Just to bring you up to date on the drape issue—as if the new drapes were not bad enough, Betty came home Saturday with a stack of wallpaper books.

Calling the Pan Back . . .

REMEMBER A LONG TIME AGO WHEN I told you there was a pin-hole leak in the oil pan and Dan, Bondo, and I fixed it by inserting a sheet metal screw and little rubber O-ring? Well, now's my chance to find out what that was all about. I clean out the oil pan and find that while The Woodpecker was sitting all those years rusting, water had collected in the oil pan. Right where the water met the oil floating on its surface, there is some pitting. One of those pits is deep enough that it penetrated the metal of the pan and caused the leak. I clean the pan, and the leak, and run some hot solder into the pitting. I'm not very good at this, so it's a little messy, but I smooth it out, seal up the hole, and call it good—after all, this is inside the pan. No one will ever notice a thing once I file off the little bubble of solder protruding through the hole. I try the pan with water. It's sealed tightly.

Putting the pan upside down on the fairly level concrete floor, I can see that the lip that fastens to the block is uneven. In fact, in a couple places—notably, at the back of the pan where my oil leak was—it twists up a good quarter inch. I tap it back to level with a brass hammer, hoping that will solve my leak problems.

I find the hood I took off the tractor almost two years ago and clean it up, find new mounting bolts, and get ready to put it on. Mostly the hood is a matter of window dressing, but I have to do what I can to make her look good for her party. She's not much to look at as it is. Remember, this is not a restoration tractor. No one who looks at this thing is going to consider it attractive unless they know the story—for example, what it looked like two years ago when Jim Stromp scraped it off his truck into the yard.

I clean the engine block and oil pan surfaces in preparation of remounting the pan. Next I loosen the lugs on the back wheels in anticipation of putting on the new ones. Then I re-install the valve cover. Cindy Clawford edges toward me, building up her courage to visit me and the tractor, and then, the moment I love, at a signal known only to her, she leaps frantically away as if I were about to pinch her head off. Women!

Day 60 hours	3.0
Total project hours	220.0

Smashing Tunes

WELSCH WEATHER REPORT

Fall is well underway. It's a rainy, cool day.

I DRIVE INTO ST. PAUL, NEBRASKA, and pick up the new tires and wheels from Vern. Turns out, we got a better deal than we thought, and the tires are really very nice. My tire problems are fairly well taken care of, I would guess, pretty much for the rest of my tractor work career.

I pull off the old, rotten, leaking tires and roll them out to the yard, a shaky, frightening process. Then I roll two of the new ones into the shop—much less of a job because I didn't have them filled with fluid. All this excitement scares Cindy half to death, which is probably a good thing because she has now become a part of the family, and I would get into real trouble if I squashed her under a tractor tire.

That is not an altogether unlikely scenario. While working at mounting the left wheel, it gets away from me and falls right into my new CD player—breaking it. Jeez, suddenly the new tires get real expensive real fast. But I get the new wheels and tires on without too much trouble—or at least none that I am aware of at that point.

I fasten down the hood and begin preparations to remount the oil pan. The party approaches, and I'm eager to get this thing sewed up. I put the end crankshaft cap back on (I took it off to see if I could spot a leak in the rear seal), torque it down, and tie it with safety tire.

Day 61 hours	3.0
Total project hours	223.0

Wrestling Fenders

WELSCH WEATHER REPORT

The chill of winter is near. A cold day. I stoke the shop stove with the first fire of the season.

I HAVE SET ASIDE THE ENTIRE DAY to work on The Woodpecker, hoping to finish things up for the re-commissioning party. Cindy is delighted to see me, demonstrating that by ricocheting in and out of her little cat door a couple dozen times at full speed. I have two goals in mind for today: 1) finish the oil pan re-mounting, and 2) mount the fenders. I apply a thin layer of gasket compound on the cleaned oil pan, which is still a pretty wavy bit of iron. I hope the gasket and compound will seal it up on the block. I get out the gaskets and . . . what's this little envelope? I recognize everything else and know where it goes, but the two little pieces of cardboard in the separate envelope baffle me.

I turn to my parts book. One of the first major investments I made in tractor work was a parts book for the Allis WC. It cost me $60 at an Allis dealer's auction sale, and it proved well worth the investment. These days you can buy reproductions of parts manuals for a fraction of that cost; I can't imagine a tractor restoration proceeding without this basic resource. I look at the crankcase page. There are the two little gasket tabs: they fit around the felt seal at the back cap. Hmmm. Could it be that omission of these tabs causing a leak back there? I take off the rear crankshaft cap, put the little tabs in place, and replace and retorque the cap. Here's hoping that works.

While the gasket sealer sets up a little on the pan, I go to work on the fenders. Bondo gave me a real bad time about taking so long to do jobs that should only take an hour or so, but once again I realize the enormous difference between his mechanicking and mine: I work with old iron. For one thing, bolts have been stuck longer in my projects—sometimes by decades or even generations, but there is also the gauge factor. The mere task of carrying an Allis WC fender the hundred yards or so from the storage pile to the shop is a major labor because the fender is solid iron and weighs about 75 pounds. Now, if it is a job to carry it, getting it in place is even more of a task. Then comes the misery of holding it into position while inserting bolts and applying washers and nuts.

I spot immediately the lesson for the day: If you are going to put fenders on an Allis Chalmers WC, be sure you do that before you put on wheels and tires. I can see I will be able to work around the tires to get two of the mounting bolts in place, but the third, large top bolt that goes through the fender and the brake case is impossible to get to. Impossible. I simply don't have time to dismount the tires, put in that one bolt, and remount the tire . . . on each side. So, for one of the first times in the two-year history of this project, I have to shrug my shoulders and say, "Good enough. I'll put in that third bolt when I take the wheels off."

But not until I spend almost three hours trying to get that one blasted bolt in place.

I take a break between fenders to lift the pan in place and tighten it down. Once again I bless the guy who invented Snap-Ups, little plastic devices that let you easily lift an oil pan into place and then hold it until you put in the bolts. All the while I'm doing this, I pray that somewhere along the line I have taken care of the problem. Since I never spotted anything that was the clear source of the leak, I can't be sure I've solved anything.

Then I turn to the other fender. In a way, I'm lucky with this one because the cast-iron brake lid on this, the left side, has its little fender-mounting ear broken off so I don't have to worry about the third, behind-the-tire bolt. But I quickly run into another problem. Lying on my back, trying to juggle the massive iron fender in place, while then inserting a bolt, sliding on a washer, and starting a nut on it, I find that for some reason I can get one bolt started, but the other never comes closer than an inch to where it should be. I sweat, wrestle, and cuss for a couple hours at this before I stop and begin the staring process.

The best I can guess is that this fender has been banged, bruised, battered, and bent so often that it is twisted out of shape. I take it off—almost as much a job as trying to put the brute on—and lay it on the floor. It is indeed bent and warped. I press it back into rough shape by standing on it, lifting it into place (not unlike an Olympic bench-press, I might note), and trying again. I fasten the front mounting bolt and move to the rear. It is still 3/4 of an inch off.

Time for serious iron bending, I decide. So, I hook a come-along cable winch to the underside of the front of the fender, pass it under the back axle to the rear of the fender and snug it up a little. Aha!

Now it is only a half inch off. I give the ratchet handle a couple more pulls. The holes line up. I slip in the bolt, slide on the washer, and start the nut. I tighten the nut. The fenders are on.

Before I clean up, kiss Cindy goodnight, and close the shop, I take a quick inventory. As far as I can see, the only things left to do are put oil in the crankcase and look for leaks ("Please, God . . . "), mount the fly-wheel cover, re-fasten the front engine mount bracket I had to take off to get to the oil pan, check for a leak in the oil filter mounting bracket, and . . . well, maybe that's it. If I have any spare time, I may try to get that broken bolt out of the clutch inspection port mount. I think I'll call Melvin Nelson to see if he wouldn't like to drop by Saturday before the party to make sure we get the thing running again. (Boy, would it be embarrassing if I couldn't get it running!)

I go to the house after seven hours of hard work (I'll bet I laid down on the floor and got back up a good 200 times during the day), so sore I head straight to the hot tub and the Tylenol bottle. Linda may have been right when she said I should have a hobby that doesn't weigh quite so much. I call Melvin and he says to call him if I have trouble.

Day 62 hours	6.0
Total project hours	229.0

DAY 63

Dressed and Ready to Go

WELSCH WEATHER REPORT

A gorgeous fall day. The warm sun blazes on the trees now in full color. I think The Woodpecker is nearing completion. Good thing, because this is the day before the party celebrating her re-entry into the world of run-

I SNUG UP THE PAN BOLTS, INSTALL the fly wheel cover, wipe off a few oil smudges, top up the radiator coolant, snug up the oil filter holder, roll the tractor out of the shop, fill up the tank with gas, empty the fuel sediment to get rid of a few little bits of dirt, pour in oil, and . . . and . . . and . . . and that's it. I can't think of anything else. I check my lists. I walk around the tractor checking, thinking, trying to remember loose ends. Nothing. Good grief, is this really it?! I crawl under her one last time, to Cindy Clawford's utter amazement. No drips. Nothing loose. Nothing missing.

I go to town to check on party arrangements—the champagne is cold, the crackers, cheese, and sandwich meats are sliced and ready. I stand around trying to think of what to do next. But there isn't anything. The Woodpecker is finished. I probably should start her just to be sure I won't be embarrassed on The Big Day, but maybe I can do that tomorrow just before the party. She ran before; surely she'll run fine tomorrow.

I sweep out the shop, put down clean cardboard on the floor, clean off my work bench in case any of the party guests come by to see it, put away tools, pick up scraps, and . . . keep looking out at The Woodpecker sitting in the autumn sun. With hood and fenders reinstalled, she's darn near pretty. Yes, all the dents, scrapes, and scratches are still there. Sure, a paint job would be nice, but my only goal, only aim was to get her running again . . . and I've done that. Nonetheless,

after two years in the shop, and all those trials and troubles, she does look pretty in my eyes.

After a morning's work I go in to finish up office work and make further party plans.

> Day 63 hours   3.0
> (Probably the last I'll spend on The
>   Woodpecker)
> Total project hours   232.0
>   (The Grand Total)

DAY 64

Epilogue

WELSCH WEATHER REPORT

Sunshine. Warmth. A perfect day. Perhaps the tractor gods approve.

I CONCENTRATE ON PREPARATIONS FOR the party. In town I buy orange crepe streamers to decorate the tractor for the Grand Entry. (Since this is October, there's no problem finding orange crepe!) I double check the food and drink arrangements, pull three other Allis Chalmers out of the machine shed—the WD, Antonia's C, and good ol' Sweet Allis, my first Allis Chalmers WC. In the house I get out my Persian Orange overalls and T-shirt and clean up. (P.O. is the official Allis Chalmers color.)

By afternoon everything is ready. Mick Maun, his wife Kathy, and daughter Liz arrive from Lincoln, and we chat a while, and then Dave Mowitz and his brother Bryan knock. At almost the same moment, Dan Selden arrives, and before long we are out in the yard looking over tractors, admiring once again the lack of wet spots under The Woodpecker. We decorate her with streamers of orange crepe, and I haul out a chain so we can pull-start her for the grand parade into town. While Mick goes in the house to change into *his* orange outfit, Dan asks why I'm not crank-starting the new machine. "Well, she's pretty stiff, what with new bearings and seals, and I don't want to break my arm, and I just thought it would be easier and cleaner to pull-start her, and if she's reluctant—I haven't started her since I closed her up this last time, after all—we'd get all tired and sweaty, and . . . "

Dan steps up to the tractor, pulls out the crank, and shoves it into place. "Couldn't hurt to give it try. Mind?" he asks, pointing at the crank.

"Help yourself," I laugh.

He takes that position peculiar to tractor crankers and mule doctors and gives a mighty heave. The engine turns, but more importantly, it *pops*.

Wow. He looks at me meaningfully and re-assumes the position. He heaves again. The tractor starts and runs, smoothly. We laugh over the roar of the engine . . . and then it dies.

"Jeez, I forgot to open the gas petcock," I snort, and open the valve, letting fuel into the line. "Now we'll probably have a heck of time getting her running."

Without a word, Dan tries again, and again it starts, and again it runs, and again it runs smoothly, and this time it just gets smoother. No coolant drips from the block radiator, hose, or block. No oil drips from the rear of the engine. She just sits there and runs. Dan jumps on the WD and starts her up. Dave takes the C, Mick climbs aboard Sweet Allis. We start into town, a grand parade of Persian Orange driven by grown men grinning like idiots, led by The Woodpecker, virtually purring, decked out in streamers and festoons of festive crepe. Her proudest moment since she rolled off the assembly line in Wisconsin.

Revelers are already gathered at the tavern, and they come pouring into the street at the unmistakable roar of four old Allises pulling up. There are congratulations, suggestions, memories, laughter, critiques, photos, good-natured insults. For a quarter hour every one stands out in the middle of the town's main street and admires, and then we turn off the tractors and adjourn to the inside of the tavern for food, toasts, and more laughter. There are comments about those who aren't there.

The week before the party, invited guests began to call to confirm their reservations for what was clearly going to be a grand start for the Dannebrog social season. Verne Holoubek was already tied up, but that's understandable. Lee Klancher, friend and editor of my books with Motorbooks, was a major disappointment because his excuse was so flimsy—he had to go to a wedding. Okay, it was his own wedding, but it was early enough in the day that he and the bride still could have made it to Nebraska for the evening. I mean, jeez, he was going to have to take her somewhere special anyway, so why not to the big tractor party for The Woodpecker? I even suggested that we could save some money by combining the wedding reception with the tractor party, thus allowing us to buy $2.50 a bottle champagne rather than the $1.99 stuff. (Lee said he had arranged for a "box" champagne for the wedding.)

Scott Leisinger swore he would be here, mostly because it's his anniversary and his wife announced she wanted to go to "some exotic desert place where the natives dress in colorful garb and speak a strange language," which, as Scott was quick to point out, sounded to him like a fairly straightforward description of Dannebrog.

Don Hochstetler was off fishing for the weekend, others were at the football game in Lincoln (a pretty weak excuse, in my opinion), but there are plenty of good folks on hand to make the evening a joyous one. I am shocked when I look outside and find that it's getting dark . . . two hours have already passed and we need to get the tractors back to the farm before it's so dark that driving on public roads without lights becomes dangerous. We mount up and drive out of town, me feeling a trifle teary-eyed about The Woodpecker at this point. I pat her on the gas tank as if she were a good horse. In a way she is.

Back at the farm we put the tractors to bed, stand around the shop talking a while, and then call it an evening. Before I go to the house, I check The Woodpecker again, putting a jar over the exhaust pipe to prevent cold, moist air from entering the engine. I pat her one last time before I go in.

And Finally . . .

In the morning Mick and his family are up early with us (since they're from out of town, they stay over) and before long, Dan and Bondo join us for coffee and rolls and a reprise of the party and tractor work. We concur it was a grand event. When they leave, Linda goes out to her studio to paint, and Antonia gets down to her homework.

Outside, I take the streamers off The Woodpecker and check her for leaks. Dry and clean. What a feeling! And what's in store for her now? Well, for me, the fun is now over. I have tractors I use for work, and tractors I like to drive into town for fun. I imagine I'll use The Woodpecker as part of the honor guard for any future tractor recommissioning parties . . . that would be nice. But to be honest, her debut is also her farewell as far as I'm concerned. I have some thoughts about donating her to a good cause, for antique tractor restoration and preservation, but that remains to be seen. Heaven knows, she'd be a great prize for a fund-raising raffle. After this book, she's the best documented tractor ever, anywhere.

Or she may be my first effort at a *real* restoration—sheet metal, paint job, decals, all that. Then she would really make a fine prize for a charity raffle. Yeah, that's it: when I'm ready to do some body work and painting, The Woodpecker will be the first to receive the new make-up on her lovely old skin. She deserves it, after all.

I pat her on the fender once again and repark the WC, WD, and Sweet Allis, so I have plenty of room in the machine shed. Somewhere along here I walk past the row of junk machines I have lined up for future work. For some reason, my eye keeps going to a WD a fellow not far from here gave me in exchange for a set of the various books I've authored. The WD is a fairly simple little machine but still, it's a lot more complicated than my usual WCs. This one has three flat tires and the engine seems to be stuck. But it wouldn't be much trouble to get it out of its place and into the shop. I'll have to give it more thought.

I put away a few more things and take another look at the WD at the same time. I did pick up a bunch of WD parts from the Jeffries when they were here last spring. Actually, it wouldn't take much to pull the machine out of the shed so I could get a better look at it. I go into the house and pull Antonia (who comes reluctantly) out to help me. She gets on the WD while I pull it out with the other WD. Heck, while I'm at it, and Antonia is in the seat, I pull it over close to the shop.

I give a couple tentative tugs at the wheel lugs to see if I'll have any trouble—when I get around to it—getting work wheels on it so I can pull it into the shop. Hmmm. Not only are the lugs stuck, the wheels are not at all like WC wheels. I may not even be able to use my work wheels on this job. I wonder if the WD will go through the shop door with the back wheels set this wide. I measure. Just barely. With a little care, it might go in. Just to test things, I hook up the power winch in the shop. I pull the tractor up to the door. It goes through with inches to spare. (Later, when I want to pull The Woodpecker under the roof into the vacant spot left by this WD, I fuss because I can't find anyone willing to crawl up onto a tractor seat and give me a pull-start. Finally, in desperation, I push the crank onto The Woodpecker's crank shaft and give it a turn. It starts. Just like that. Once again, tears come to my eyes in wonder at this ol' girl who was my companion in the shop for so many months.)

I take a look at this new collection of rust and stuck parts. Well, the WD's engine is indeed stuck, and the wheels are ruined. The oil pan is battered and probably leaks. But I suppose if I get those wheels off and the tractor up on stands and pull the head and the pan and clean up every-thing, well, then . . .

By now I guess you have the idea. What I see before me in this pile of rusted junk and rotten rubber is a whole new set of adventures and friend-ly encounters, a year or two of fun and fuss, and maybe even somewhere down the line another party. Suddenly the sadness of seeing The Woodpecker done, the vacant echo of the empty shop bay, the curious feeling of having no problems of stuck bolts and stuck engines ahead of me is gone. I'd tell you more, but I don't have time right now. I need to get this PTO unit off and find out what's keeping it from going into gear when I pull on the lever. Maybe it's this little broken thing here. There's a bit of cold in the air. It may snow in the next few days, and even today a fire in the shop stove would feel good.

" . . . As the saying goes, when the only tool you have is a hammer,
every problem looks like a nail."
Judge Sol Wachter, *The New Yorker*, p. 73, July 15, 1996